Nature in
East Anglia

S. A. Manning F.L.S.

Nature in
East Anglia

Foreword by Robert Dougall M.B.E.

WORLD'S WORK LTD
The Windmill Press Kingswood Tadworth Surrey

Other books by S. A. Manning

BROADLAND NATURALIST
The Soman-Wherry Press

THE RIGHT WAY TO UNDERSTAND THE COUNTRYSIDE
Right Way Books (Andrew George Elliot)

BAKERS AND BREAD
Basil Blackwell

TREES AND FORESTS
Basil Blackwell

THE LADYBIRD BOOK OF BUTTERFLIES, MOTHS AND OTHER INSECTS
Wills & Hepworth

SYSTEMATIC GUIDE TO FLOWERING PLANTS OF THE WORLD
Museum Press

THE INSECT WORLD
World's Work

THE WOODLAND WORLD
World's Work

THE NATURALIST IN SOUTH-EAST ENGLAND
David & Charles

Copyright © 1976 S. A. Manning
Printed in Great Britain by
Fletcher & Son Ltd, Norwich
SBN 437 09500 2

To all who promote the work of
The Norfolk Naturalists' Trust
and to the memory of its founder,
Dr. Sidney Long,
and those who supported him
during the early years of
nature conservation.

ACKNOWLEDGEMENTS

The author and publishers are indebted to the following for permission to use black and white illustrations on the following pages:
Hallam Ashley, F.R.P.S. 16, 17, 21, 33, 42, 52.
Cambridge University Collection: copyright reserved 19, 20, 22, 24, 26, 27, 46.
Leonard and Marjorie Gayton 25.
G. St J. Hollis 18, 23, 28, 34, 38, 44, 49, 58–61, 63–65, 68, 82, 96, 109.
The late John Markham, F.R.P.S., F.Z.S. (J. Allan Cash Ltd.,) 31, 36, 39, 51, 54, 62, 66, 70–81, 83–91, 98–104, 110–114, 117–137.
Ministry of Agriculture, Fisheries and Food: Crown Copyright, reproduced by permission of the Controller of Her Majesty's Stationery Office 115–116.
They are also grateful to Bruce Coleman Limited who supplied the transparencies by the following photographers opposite the pages listed.
Jane Burton, 120, 128, 134.
John Markham, F.R.P.S., F.Z.S., 32.
S. C. Bisserot, F.R.P.S., 64
Hans Reinhard, 80, 112.
Also to Tony Stone Associates Limited who supplied the frontispiece.
The map on page 14 is Crown Copyright. Based on Geological Survey material and reproduced by permission of the Controller, Her Majesty's Stationery Office.

Contents

EAST ANGLIA

North Sea

The Wash

Great Yarmouth
Gorleston-on-Sea
Lowestoft
Kessingland
Covehithe
Caister-on-Sea
Winterton-on-Sea 64
Horsey
Horsey Mere 29
Martham
Ormesby
Filby Broad
Breydon Water 10
Decoy Broad
Fritton 21
Oulton Broad
Suffolk Wild Life and County Park 50
Benacre
Beccles
R. Bure
A143
A146
A145
A144
Happisburgh
Bacton
Mundesley
Hickling Broad 25
A149
Barton 3
Barton Broad
Hoveton 11
Ranworth
R. Thurne
B1152
R. Yare
Surlingham
Hardley
Hardley and Norton Marshes
Rockland St. Mary
Loddon
(A144)
Bungay 42
R. Waveney
Harleston
Wensum Forest 61
R. Ant
Coltishall
Wroxham
Rackheath
NORWICH
A47
A146
North Walsham
R. Bure
A140
Cromer
Sheringham
Beeston Regis
West Runton
Felbrigg 19
4 63
A149
Aylsham 6
Blickling Hall
Buxton Heath
Wymondham
A11
Diss
A140
Weybourne
32
Holt
B1354
Bawdeswell
Gt. Witchingham 39
A47
R. Yare
B1108
B1077
Banham 2
South Lopham
Knettishall 34 44
A1066
Cley-next-the-Sea
Salthouse 14
Swanton Novers 52
A1067
R. Wensum
Dereham
Scarning
Scoulton Mere
Scoulton
Attleborough
A1075
Kilverstone
33 Thetford
A1075
Blakeney Point
Blakeney 5
Wells
Little Walsingham
Thursford
A148
B1065
Fakenham
Hockham
East Wretham 18
Thetford Forest
53 54
Thetford Heath
Holkham Bay 26
Holkham
Scolt Head I. 48
Brancaster 8
Titchwell 55
B1355
Burnham Market
Massingham Heath
A148
Swaffham
Watton
R. Wissey
BRECKLAND
Weeting 59
Brandon 9
58
Wangford Warren
A1065
Lakenheath
Brancaster Bay
Holme 28 27
Ringstead
Heacham
Snettisham 49
Dersingham 15
Sandringham 47
Roydon
46
LEZIATE FEN
East Winch
R. Nar
Shouldham 36
A122
A134
Hunstanton
Castle Rising
A149
A47
A10
Downham Market
R. Wissey
Little Ouse R.
A1101
King's Lynn
Terrington St. Clement
A17
Great Ouse R.
New Bedford River
60
Wisbech
Norwich
From the Midlands & the North
Old Bedford River
A10
Ely

N O R T H   S E A

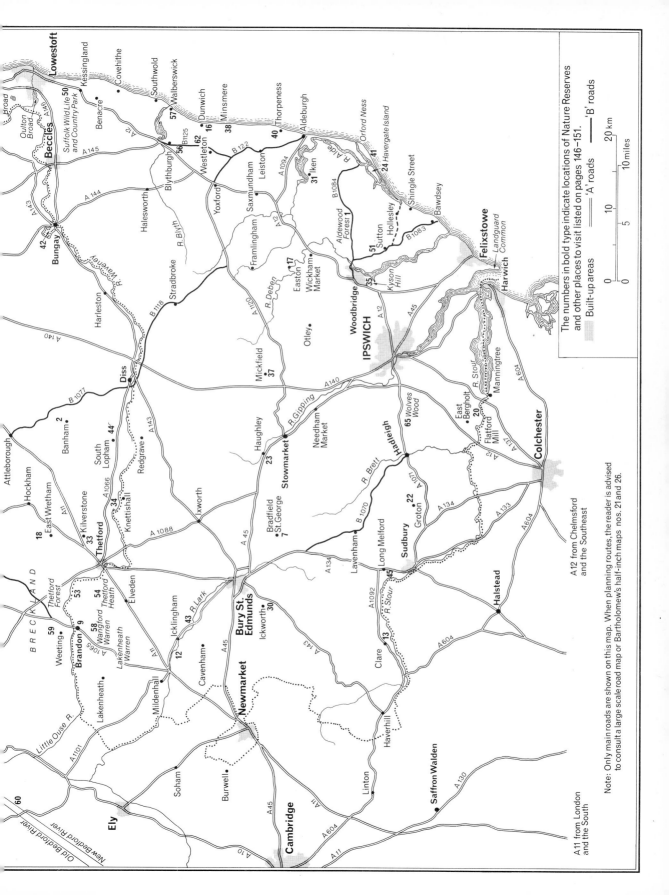

The numbers in bold type indicate locations of Nature Reserves and other places to visit listed on pages 146–151.

'A' roads
'B' roads

Built-up areas

Note: Only main roads are shown on this map. When planning routes, the reader is advised to consult a large scale road map or Bartholomews half-inch maps nos. 21 and 26.

A12 from Chelmsford and the Southeast

A11 from London and the South

Foreword by Robert Dougall M.B.E.

East Anglia can mean so many different things to different people. To me it is, above all, the marshes in winter when sea and sky are one – the inside of an oyster shell – and the purple reed-tops tilt towards the sea.

Others may think first of the flat, black earth of the Fens, the shallow lakes and winding rivers of the Broads, the dark forests and what is left of Breckland, the estuaries and salt marshes near the coast or of the dunes and shingly beaches. In the solitary places a strange, timeless feeling hangs in the air: primeval man himself would find few changes in many a tussocky swamp.

Poor communications over the centuries have lent the region a kind of insularity. Indeed, the ancestors of present-day fenmen lived out their lives on the islands of an inland sea, until the Dutchman, Cornelius Vermuyden came in the 17th century to apply himself to the serious job of drainage. Perhaps this is how the 'fen-tigers' got their special kind of toughness and independence. Another result of this comparative isolation has been the survival of an unusually wide variety of flora and fauna.

Now, at last, the 20th century is catching up: motorways, over-spill towns, factories, power-stations and pylons are posing a threat to the age-old order of things. It is therefore all the more important that as many people as possible should become aware of their unique heritage and take a personal interest in its conservation before it is too late.

That is why this admirable and comprehensive work by S. A. Manning is so timely and why I feel honoured at having been invited to write the foreword. In any case, I owe East Anglia a great debt: it was here on the deserted beaches and among the reed-beds, which are like another sea, that I first had my eyes opened to many a natural delight. The mystery to me now is how I had come to live half my life with such dull, unseeing eyes.

My awakening came just after the war when my wife Nan and I inherited a tiny holiday cottage on the Suffolk coast. We could scarcely have come to a better place at a better time. Ornithologists were in a state of excitement because a few miles down the coast at Minsmere that elegant black and white wader the avocet was found to be breeding again after an absence from Britain of over a hundred years. As a coastal defence measure, the grazing marshes had been inundated during the war and, when the sluices began operating again, a large expanse of reeds and marshland had developed. It was there that four pairs of avocets were found. The Royal Society for the Protection of Birds, which then had only a few thousand members, lost no time and in 1948 the local landowner Captain Stuart Ogilvie agreed to lease 1,500 acres as a sanctuary. Another four pairs were found to be nesting on Havergate Island in Orfordness and this too was acquired as a reserve.

Over the years, thanks to dedicated care and skilful management, the avocet has now become well established again with successful breeding colonies at both places. This must surely be one of the greatest triumphs in British ornithological history.

I have also been a witness to the creation at Minsmere of one of the most exciting and significant conservation successes in the whole of Europe. About twelve years ago, terns were finding it impossible to breed on the beach owing to increased pressure from holidaymakers. The idea was then conceived of clearing a fifty acre area of salt-marsh, and bull-dozing out a shallow lagoon, studded with islands, to provide threatened species with secure nesting conditions.

I recall strenuous, invigorating sessions spent in the construction of these islands and the R.S.P.B. were fortunate in having a single-minded, and dedicated conservationist as Senior Warden, Herbert Axell, to nurture and direct the project. As a result, 1,500 pairs of breeding birds were added to the reserve and it is now a favourite staging-point for hosts of waders on their great journeyings across the world. Also at almost every season of the year it is a birdwatcher's delight.

Minsmere has resolved one of the great dilemmas of conservation: how to provide the right breeding conditions for some of Britain's rarest and shiest birds, the marsh-harrier among them, and yet permit many thousands of watchers a year to observe them by means of covered walks and hides.

We must hope that East Anglia's development will in all respects be carefully controlled. Fortunately, it is taking place at a time when there is, partly thanks to natural history programmes on radio and television, a great upsurge of interest. The R.S.P.B., of which I had the honour to be President from 1970–75, now numbers some quarter of a million members.

I have written mainly of birds because I know them best, but this book also deals with the geology of the region; it tells of trees and plants, mammals, amphibians, reptiles and insects and, what's more, tells you where you can see them.

Smaller than the R.S.P.B., but great in influence, is the Norfolk Naturalists' Trust to which this work is happily dedicated to mark its Golden Jubilee Year. How delighted Dr. Sidney Long its founder would have been to know of the progress since 1926, when he first acquired those four hundred acres of marshes at Cley.

The author, in his schooldays, had the pleasure of knowing the good Doctor. S. A. Manning is, of course, a Norwich man, a distinguished naturalist and former teacher of Biology and has lived in or near East Anglia all his life with the exception of travel in the Royal Air Force during the war.

As we turn the pages of his book, let us hope too, that some of East Anglia's remoteness will remain. In Thoreau's words:
'We need the tonic of wildness –
In wildness is the preservation of the world'.

East Anglia: sub-regions and reserves

East Anglia, which, for the purpose of this book, means Norfolk and Suffolk, lies on the drier, sunnier side of Britain and includes some of the country's best soils. An important centre of arable farming whose major crops include wheat, barley and sugar-beet, it is nevertheless an outstanding area for nature and naturalist alike.

The Fens

At one time the low plateau of East Anglia was largely isolated from the rest of Britain, one barrier being the watery wastes of the Fens at its western edge. Drainage made this land of 'much water and few reeds' into a fertile farming area. But it still has many features of interest to the naturalist. Pride of place must be given to the Ouse Washes, a habitat of black-tailed godwit and ruff and an internationally important wildfowl refuge.

Lying between the Old and New Bedford Rivers, two great artificial drainage channels, the Ouse Washes form a flood storage plain half a mile wide and 21 miles in length. Winter flooding attracts thousands of migratory wildfowl, including mallard, pintail, shoveler, teal, wigeon, and Bewick's, whooper and mute swans, while in spring receding flood waters leave the land soft and moist and many birds feed and breed there. The Royal Society for the Protection of Birds (RSPB), the Cambridgeshire and Isle of Ely Naturalists' Trust (CAMBIENT), and the Wildfowl Trust, which publish details of visiting arrangements and positions of hides, have acquired parts of these washlands and are, in fact, the largest landowners in the area. Unlike the reserves of the other two bodies, which are in Cambridgeshire, the Welney Wildfowl Refuge of the Wildfowl Trust is in Norfolk, the assembly point for visitors being at Pintail House on the south-east side of the Washes, $1\frac{1}{4}$ miles north-east of the suspension bridge.

The Greensand Belt

Also in the west of Norfolk is the Greensand belt, a low ridge of sandy land extending from Snettisham in the north to the neighbourhood of Downham Market in the south. Besides several large sporting estates, this sub-region includes heathland, birchwoods, and a number of fen commons. Roydon Common is one of the large unenclosed commons in the area, and part of it forms a reserve of the Norfolk Naturalists' Trust (NNT). Situated about $4\frac{1}{2}$ miles north-east of King's Lynn and on the south side of the main King's Lynn – Grimston road, it supports dry heath with bracken and heather, wet heath, bog, reedswamp and a very damp wood. Not far away, East Winch Common, another NNT reserve, includes wet acid heathland, birchwood and other habitats. Between Roydon and East Winch, besides the Gaywood River, which flows through the Greensand belt, are Sugar, Derby and Leziate Fens, commons scheduled as Sites of Special Scientific Interest (SSSI) by the Nature Conservancy Council, largely because of their great botanical interest.

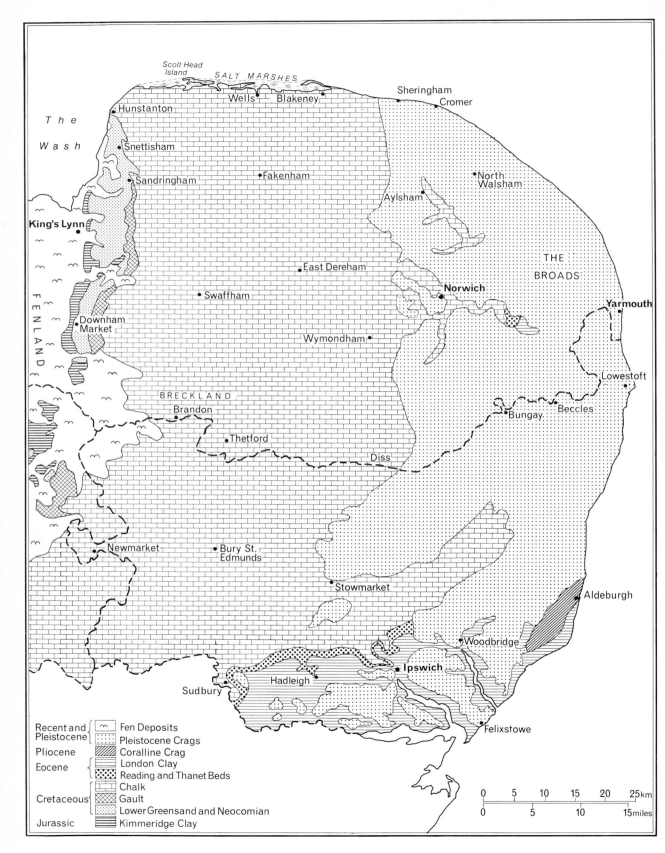

Scolt Head
Island
SALT MARSHES
Wells • Blakeney
Sheringham •
Cromer

The
Wash
Hunstanton
• Snettisham
North
Walsham
• Fakenham
Aylsham
Sandringham

King's Lynn
• East Dereham
THE
BROADS

FENLAND
• Swaffham
Norwich •
Yarmouth

Downham
Market
Wymondham •
Lowestoft

BRECKLAND
Bungay
Beccles •

Brandon •
Thetford
Diss

Newmarket
Bury St.
Edmunds
Stowmarket •
Aldeburgh

Woodbridge

Hadleigh
Ipswich
Sudbury
Felixstowe

Recent and Pleistocene		Fen Deposits
		Pleistocene Crags
Pliocene		Coralline Crag
Eocene		London Clay
		Reading and Thanet Beds
Cretaceous		Chalk
		Gault
		Lower Greensand and Neocomian
Jurassic		Kimmeridge Clay

0   5   10   15   20   25km

0   5   10   15miles

To the east of the Fenland and the Greensand Belt, some 400 square miles of south-west Norfolk and north-west Suffolk are occupied by the Breckland. This sub-region of light, dry, sandy or sandy-calcareous soils, where rainfall is low, is not only exceptionally liable to summer drought but may have frosts in any month of the year. These and other factors combine to make Breckland an area of great ecological interest. The name of the district was created by W. G. Clarke in 1894 from the word breck, meaning a piece of heathland which was broken up for cultivation at certain times and allowed to revert to waste at others. At one time it was more profitable to abandon the brecks to rabbits (millions of rabbits!), but subsequent changes of land use in the sub-region have brought even more drastic changes.

Today large parts of Breckland are covered with pinewoods established by the Forestry Commission, others are used as military training areas and for other defence purposes, while reclamation and improvement have turned thousands of acres of 'waste' ground and heath into productive pastures and arable land. At times these changes have exposed serious conflicts of attitude to the light, sandy soils of Breckland. One such case occurred during the successful agricultural experiment in the Suffolk Breckland, in which lucerne, a drought-resistant herbage plant and fertility builder on poor soils, played a vital part. This was Lord Iveagh's two years' dispute with the Forestry Commission who wanted to acquire part of the Elveden Estate for tree-planting. A provisional compulsory purchase order was made, but in 1951 a Select Committee of the House of Commons unanimously decided to throw out the Confirming Bill, thus leaving Lord Iveagh free to continue farming and reclaiming the land. The successful opposition of the commoners to attempts to afforest Lakenheath Warren left nearly 1,000 acres of unspoilt dry breck heath over which there are some sheep-grazing rights. This half of the Warren is an SSSI, the other being an airfield.

Fortunately there were, during the years of changing land use and conflict, those who appreciated the importance of retaining some of the unspoilt heath and other habitats as nature reserves. Thanks to these pioneers of conservation, a few isolated areas remain, reminders of the great stretches of open rolling heath and wilderness that have disappeared in Breckland.

East Wretham Heath, an SSSI covering some 360 acres of heath and woodland, was acquired in 1938 by the NNT. This reserve includes Langmere and Ringmere, whose water level shows considerable long-term fluctuations. The remaining heathland meres – Fowlmere, Punchbowl Mere, and Home Mere – are similarly affected and, like the others, dry out from time to time. The unique hydrological character of these meres was recognised by engineers studying the relationship between

Langmere, a distinctive feature of East Wretham Heath Nature Reserve. With the other heathland meres of Breckland it shares a unique hydrological character.

the level of water in the meres and that of ground water in the surrounding chalk, work undertaken to determine whether the meres would suffer irreparable damage if, in dry seasons, a considerable quantity of water was taken from the chalk for river regulation.

The NNT received as gifts in the 1940s Weeting Heath (343 acres) and Thetford Heath (250 acres), now National Nature Reserves, the status accorded to reserves established by the Nature Conservancy Council in cooperation with owners and tenants. Visitors to these reserves must hold Nature Conservancy Council permits (Apply East Anglia Region office). Much of Cavenham Heath National Nature Reserve (376 acres), mostly typical breck heathland, is open to the public for whose convenience a small car-park and picnic site are provided at Temple Bridge (N.C.C. permits *are* needed for Ash Plantation, Tuddenham Poor's Heath and Cavenham Poor's Heath). Wangford Warren (38 acres), the property of the Suffolk Trust for Nature Conservation (STNC) and an SSSI, is of considerable interest, being a reserve where active erosion is being maintained. Several smaller Breckland reserves have been scheduled as SSSIs and details of their location are supplied to members of the County Trusts for Nature Conservation.

In Thetford Forest (83 square miles) the Forestry Commission provides forest trails, walks and picnic areas, and there are a number of public bridleways and footpaths. Naturalists should take full advantage of these facilities, but only after studying the Thetford Forest guide map and related publications.

Chalk   Over much of East Anglia chalk, already mentioned in connection

with the Breckland meres, underlies boulder clays, sands and gravels, superficial rocks whose thickness varies from place to place, often considerably within a small area. These conditions can have a marked effect on plant life. For example, after May drought at Gooderstone in Breckland, barley yielded 7 cwt per acre where water-holding chalk loam was within 1 foot of the surface but died completely where loamy sand was 3 feet deep.

Chalk appears at the surface mainly in the west of the region, but even there typical chalk grassland is rare. Fortunately the NNT has secured by agreement Ringstead Downs, at 26 acres the largest area of chalk grassland in Norfolk. Lying to the east of Hunstanton, this dry valley in the Middle Chalk will now be managed to ensure the conservation of the chalk plants.

At Hunstanton, whose cliffs are formed of white chalk over red chalk and carstone (Lower Greensand), there is the only section of the East Anglian coast which can in any way be called hard or rocky. But this is only one of the many interesting features of a coastline which, not without good reason, has attracted generations of naturalists.

Well-known as feeding grounds for thousands of waders, the vast mudflats of the Wash are fringed by marshes, which can be approached by turning seaward off the A 17 or A 149 a few miles out of King's Lynn. This is a bleak and desolate area where reclamation and cultivation have brought marked change. On the eastern shore of the Wash the RSPB provides a public and a members' hide at Snettisham Beach where the old gravel pits are an important roost for waders during spring tides.

The Coast

This wildfowl refuge and reserve lies between Heacham and Wolferton where large areas of land were inundated when the sea broke through the shingle bank early in 1953.

Between Hunstanton, on the prominent north-west corner of East Anglia, and Weybourne stretches the marshland coast of north Norfolk, where sand dunes are established upon offshore bars of shingle on whose landward side saltmarshes form. Conservation bodies have been active in this Area of Outstanding Natural Beauty for more than half a century.

At Holme next the Sea the Holme Dunes reserve of the NNT is an SSSI consisting of about 400 acres of foreshore, sand dunes, fresh marsh and salt marsh.

At Titchwell Marsh the RSPB owns 420 acres of low-lying land. This had been reclaimed from the sea in the nineteenth century, but was flooded again during the storms of 1949 and 1953. Behind shingle and shifting dunes are salt marsh and reedbeds intersected by creeks. In 1967 the National Trust bought 2,150 acres of beach, tidal foreshore (4½ miles), sand dunes, reclaimed marshland and saltings at Brancaster. This property is opposite Scolt Head Island, a National Nature Reserve owned by the National Trust and the NNT. Stretching about 4 miles from east to west, its width varying according to the state of the tides, the island covers 1,821 acres. A large off-shore bar, its main beach has numerous recurves, lateral or branch ridges of shingle, each once the unstable western end of the island. Reference to *Scolt Head Island* (editor: J. A. Steers), in which specialists have explained many aspects of the fauna, flora and development of this extensive dune and saltmarsh

Aerial view of Scolt Head Island, looking east. This National Nature Reserve, an extensive dune and saltmarsh system on the North Norfolk coast, is an important breeding site for terns.

system, will prepare the naturalist for his visits to this reserve.

East of Scolt Head Island is Holkham National Nature Reserve, the largest coastal National Nature Reserve in England, consisting of about 4,200 acres of coastal marshes and dunes between Burnham Overy and Stiffkey belonging to the Holkham Estate, together with 5,500 acres of intertidal sand and mud flats between Burnham Overy and Blakeney leased from the Crown Estate Commissioners. To the west of Wells-next-the-Sea the reserve consists of grazing marshes, the result of the reclamation of an extensive salt marsh during the seventeenth, eighteenth and nineteenth centuries. The pine trees growing on the dunes here were planted from about 1850 onward to stabilise them against wind erosion and to protect the reclaimed marshes from blown sand. To the east of Wells the reserve includes a large salt marsh.

Beyond the eastern boundary of Holkham National Nature Reserve is Blakeney Point, the first Norfolk nature reserve. Owned by the National Trust since 1912, this key migration point is the end of a great shingle ridge which begins at Weybourne and extends westward for nearly nine miles, its lateral ridges, as on Scolt Head Island, representing former ends. Its 1,335 acres include salt marsh, shingle beach, and sand dune, many aspects of whose fauna and flora have been closely studied. Blakeney Point can be reached by boat from Morston and Blakeney. But those who are fit enough should undertake the $3\frac{1}{2}$ mile walk over shingle from the end of the beach road at Cley: this in itself is a great experience for a naturalist.

Like Blakeney, Cley has an established place in the annals of

Sand dunes and saltmarsh at Blakeney Point, site of the first Norfolk nature reserve.

ornithology, some 300 acres of Cley Marshes Nature Reserve, an SSSI owned by the NNT, being a Statutory Bird Sanctuary where a large variety and number of birds are seen. Next to the main Cley reserve and managed as part of it, is Arnold's Marsh, a muddy feeding ground for shore birds and waders whose water level and salinity fluctuate. East Bank (access is unrestricted) affords good views of the marshes, once saltings, where in recent years new scrapes have been made to improve the facilities for waders. Adjoining Cley is Salthouse where the NNT has a management agreement with the owner over 200 acres of Salthouse marshes. Already this has resulted in the excavation of a new pool for waders and the ringing of birds of several species.

Eastward from the marshland coast cliffs of soft glacial material run from Weybourne to east of Happisburgh. Cliff falls are common, sea, wind, the action of water draining from the land, and, in places, the structure of the cliffs themselves, assisting erosion. Behind Cromer and Sheringham is a particularly attractive section of the Cromer Ridge, a prominent glacial feature composed of sands and gravels. Here, less than a mile south of West Runton station, the wooded National Trust property known locally as the Roman Camp covers $71\frac{1}{2}$ acres and, rising to more than 300 feet, includes the highest point in Norfolk. Most of the ridge between the Roman Camp and Brittons Lane is occupied by another National Trust property, Beeston Regis Heath, 37 acres of open and wooded heathland.

Beyond Happisburgh is a stretch of coast, very low in places, whose fringing dunes have not always afforded adequate protection against the

sea, and whose soft cliffs have long suffered from the forces of erosion. In 1938 the sea swept away 700 yards of sand-hills between Winterton and Horsey and flooded 7,500 acres of marshland, and in 1953 a great tidal surge resulted in much grazing land being inundated. The coastal defences have since been strengthened, but this is an area where man must ever be watchful. The coast of Broadland, a sub-region dealt with later, starts at Waxham, where scrub-covered dunes attract migrant birds, and extends as far as Lowestoft.

On this Broadland coast, a 'ness', a dune and shingle foreland, has developed in front of the old cliffs at Winterton. Here is Winterton Dunes National Nature Reserve whose 259 acres extend northward from the village for nearly two miles, reaching a maximum width of 600 yards and including heath, bog, dunes and dune slacks. Some eight miles south, behind Great Yarmoutn, is Breydon Water, the combined estuary of the Rivers Waveney, Yare and Bure, whose tidal waters, mudflats and surrounding marshes have long been famous for their bird life. Now a Local Nature Reserve because it is run by the local authority, it was once the haunt of wildfowlers and punt-gunners, a number of whom live in the books of Arthur Patterson, a distinguished field naturalist despite his pen-name of 'John Knowlittle'.

Lowestoft, at the southern end of the Broadland coast, is the most easterly point of this country and a fine migration watchpoint. Severe erosion has occurred there and at Pakefield. From the last-named place to Aldeburgh low, soft cliffs alternate with stretches of low-lying marshland whose seaward side is bounded by beaches of sand and shingle.

Breydon Water, the estuary behind Great Yarmouth, a famous haunt of waders, wildfowl and other birds.

Between Kessingland and Southwold, and separated from the sea by only a narrow beach, are Benacre, Covehithe and Easton Broads, reed-fringed open waters lying in an area of rough grazing land.

Just south-west of Southwold is Walberswick National Nature Reserve. Its 1,270 acres include the Westwood Marshes, formerly an area of drained grazing land where vast reedbeds developed after flooding was carried out during the Second World War. Angel Marshes, comprising 95 acres of tidal mudflats, and 59 acres of intertidal mudflats to the south of the River Blyth provide a refuge and feeding ground for wildfowl and waders. The higher ground, mainly heathland, was in regular use as sheep-walks until this became uneconomic in the 1930s. Formerly such heathland where sheep and rabbits grazed covered almost all of the light sandy soils of the Sandlings (as the district became known) along the east Suffolk coast.

At Westleton Heath National Nature Reserve a few miles south-west of Walberswick the Nature Conservancy Council is endeavouring to conserve plant and animal life characteristic of the Sandlings. This 117 acre reserve adjoins heathland managed by the RSPB as part of the Minsmere Bird Reserve. From the cliff-top at the south-east corner of Dunwich Heath, where the National Trust is striving to combat erosion of the sandy soil, one can look over the marsh and pools of the low-lying part of the Minsmere reserve, a place so attractive to terns and waders.

Further south, at Aldeburgh, is the northern end of Orford Ness, the largest spit on the east coast. Formed entirely of masses of shingle, it has diverted the mouth of the River Alde for a distance of about 12 miles south of its original outlet at Aldeburgh. Havergate Island lies two miles downstream from Orford. Formerly well-drained grazing land, it is managed by the RSPB as a reserve for waders, wildfowl and

other birds. Havergate Island and part of Orford beach together form Orfordness-Havergate National Nature Reserve whose area amounts to 555 acres.

On the mainland, just beyond the southern end of the spit, vast amounts of shingle have been thrown up at Shingle Street. Behind this protective barrier are grazing marshes and cultivated land. Beyond Bawdsey, with its cliffs of Red Crag and London Clay, is Felixstowe. Here the Dock and the container traffic have expanded rapidly in recent years and development is leading to great changes at Landguard Common whose south end, an important area for shingle plants, is scheduled as an SSSI. The East Anglian coast ends here, at the Orwell-Stour mouth, a haunt of waders and wildfowl.

As we progressed along its coastal boundary, from Waxham to Lowestoft, brief mention was made of Broadland. A unique sub-region, this is a land of shallow lakes (the broads) and their associated rivers, natural fens, embanked pastures, and well-farmed uplands. Often referred to as the Norfolk Broads, the vast system of waterways does, in fact, extend from east Norfolk into neighbouring Suffolk. Naturalists have long been attracted to Broadland, Sir Thomas Browne, the celebrated seventeenth-century Norwich physician, being first in a long, continuous line. Many of them have been content to observe and catalogue the animals and plants. Others have brought the penetrating light of modern science to the sub-region and have shown that the broads are not, as was long assumed, natural features but the flooded sites of great pits made in the fenland by medieval turf-cutters. The broads themselves vary considerably in shape, size, salinity and setting. Many of them are open to the public and several are managed as nature reserves, but visitors should acquaint themselves with the Broadland

Broadland

The Suffolk coast, looking north-east from Orford Haven. Here are Havergate Island and the great shingle foreland of Orford Ness.

Code (See p. 151) and avoid trespass.

Four of the Bure valley broads, namely Hoveton Great, Decoy, Ranworth and Cockshoot Broads, are within the Bure Marshes National Nature Reserve. This covers more than 1,000 acres on either side of the river between Wroxham and Ranworth, its waterways normally containing freshwater. Hoveton Great Broad is a typical by-passed broad, being originally connected with the river by openings (dykes or 'gatways') cut through the intervening fenland. Like the last-named broad, Ranworth Broad is by-passed, but it lies further from the river, access being along the sailing channel known as Ranworth Dam.

In the strongly tidal Yare valley is Surlingham Broad, a NNT reserve whose open water has a much smaller area than that shown on the map of 1839. Not far away is Rockland Broad to the north of which is Wheatfen Broad, a private nature reserve where Dr Edward Ellis has lived for many years, studying the animal and plant life and, like the previous owner, Captain Maurice Cockle, encouraging others to do likewise.

Like the two just mentioned, the Waveney valley is one of the main Broadland valleys. Here, in north-east Suffolk, is the deep broad known as Fritton Lake or Fritton Decoy, a habitat of great crested grebes and silver bream. Surrounded by well-wooded valley slopes, it looks quite different from the more typical broads, though it is believed to have originated in much the same way.

Associated with the Ant, in a secondary valley, are Barton and Alderfen Broads, NNT reserves and SSSIs. Formerly by-passing the broad, the river was artificially diverted to flow through Barton Broad itself. Often regarded as the most beautiful of the broads, Barton Broad attracts large numbers of holidaymakers and, sad to say, it has suffered in recent years from traffic and pollution. Concern over such threats to the natural history interests of Barton and Alderfen Broads led the NNT to set up a Working Party to investigate conditions at these reserves and make recommendations for their future management. Alderfen Broad is now land-locked and separated from the river by grazing marshes. It is the scene of much research by members of the University of East Anglia whose Conservation Corps has worked hard there and at other reserves, clearing rubbish and scrub and undertaking other essential tasks.

View from the tower of Ranworth church showing the broad and marshes.

Barton Broad, a
beautiful shallow lake
formed by the
flooding of medieval
turf-pits.

In the Thurne valley, another secondary valley, is the Hickling Broad
National Nature Reserve where the shallow waters of Hickling Broad
and the adjoining Whiteslea and Heigham Sounds are surrounded by
extensive reedbeds, fen and marshland. Hickling has long been famous
amongst naturalists for whom excellent bird watching and visitors'
facilities (including a water trail) are provided on the 1,361 acre NNT
property. In recent years much work has been undertaken to improve
facilities for visitors and birds alike. New hides have been erected, areas
banked and flooded, and, to encourage terns to nest, part of an island
replaced by sand and shingle. In recent years, too, there have been grim

reminders of the presence of fish, large numbers of which have had to be removed dead from the waters in the Hickling and Horsey area. This heavy mortality was apparently caused by the presence of the small alga *Prymnesium*. In an effort to restock the area, fish from other parts of Broadland have been introduced, and certain dykes are being dredged to provide a refuge for fish in the event of further outbreaks of the alga.

Like the broads of the Hickling National Nature Reserve, Martham Broad, another NNT reserve in the Thurne valley, lies in a shallow basin and, also like them, is slightly brackish. Martham was once the scene of large-scale turf production, 105,000 turves a year being produced in the early fourteenth century when Norwich Cathedral Priory alone used some 400,000 turves annually as fuel. Nowadays Martham Broad and the adjoining Starch Grass Reserve are noted for interesting plants, birds and swallowtail butterflies.

More brackish than the broads just mentioned, Horsey Mere is part of the 1,732 acre estate owned by the National Trust. Lying in a shallow

Hickling Broad where excellent bird-watching facilities are provided by the Norfolk Naturalists' Trust.

Farming districts

basin close to the sea, it is rich in bird life. Hardley Flood, 90 acres of water and marsh by the River Chet, is also of considerable ornithological interest. This area was acquired on lease by the NNT as recently as 1972, and one hopes that increasing strength and support will enable this excellent body to create even more reserves in Broadland.

Leaving this and the other distinct sub-regions of East Anglia, we must now consider the region's largely agricultural central area. Here, between the lighter soils of Breckland and the Greensand Belt on the west and those of the Cromer-Holt Ridge and the Sandlings on the east, are heavier soils chiefly derived from boulder clay. Dissected by river valleys, this central area contains many commons, meadows, small woods, hedgerows and roadside verges that serve as strongholds of wild life.

One such stronghold is Bawdeswell Heath, a 37 acre stretch of fuel allotment charity land beside the East Dereham-Reepham road in Norfolk. A popular spot with the public, this common, with its stream, fen and dry heath, supports many species of plants and birds. Along the banks of the River Waveney, charity land at Redgrave and Lopham Fens, about $5\frac{1}{2}$ miles west of Diss, had been neglected for many years when the STNC asquired it between 1964 and 1966, part by purchase, the remainder on a long lease. Formerly the poor of the parishes of Lopham and Redgrave came here to dig peat and to cut reeds and sedge, all useful materials. Now the nature reserve, some 314 acres of valley fen, is scheduled as an SSSI.

Examples of small deciduous woodlands that are being managed as nature reserves in farming districts are Groton Woods (50 acres), near Boxford and Kersey, and Bradfield Woods, near Bury St Edmunds. Groton Wood is an STNC property whose northern third formed part of the medieval manorial wood. Bradfield Woods is owned by the Society for the Promotion of Nature Reserves whose local management committee hopes to continue the 700 year old tradition of coppicing there.

Many nature reserves, picnic sites and walks are listed in an appendix, but further details of places mentioned in this book can, of course, be obtained from the offices of the Nature Conservancy Council, the Society for the Promotion of Nature Reserves, and the County Trusts, whose addresses appear on p. 152. The naturalist who prefers to use public rights of way in search of wild life should consult the appropriate Definitive Map or Ordnance Survey 1 : 50,000 map. Definitive Maps, which may be inspected at the offices of the local authorities concerned and in public libraries, are valuable legal documents. Prepared by county councils, as required by the National Parks and Access to the Countryside Act 1949, they show footpaths and bridleways separately. Under the 1949 Act, the showing of a path on a Definitive Map is conclusive evidence in law that it was a public right of way at the date the map was made (The local authority will have details of paths that have since been legally diverted or closed).

Though they are on a smaller scale, the Ordnance Survey 1 : 50,000 maps (approximately $1\frac{1}{4}$ inches to 1 mile) are very useful. They indicate in red public rights of way derived from Definitive Maps as amended by later enactments or instruments held by the Ordnance Survey on a given date.

In setting out to explore East Anglia, whether as walker, rider or motorist, the naturalist will appreciate that, while he has the right to use public roads and rights of way, he also has a duty to respect the privacy and the livelihood of those who live in the country and to observe with great care the rules governing entry to nature reserves. Where the latter are concerned, the golden rule is 'If in doubt, ask well in advance.' The duties of countrygoers are summarised in the Broadland and Country Codes (See p. 151).

Trees and other plants

Despite the fact that large parts of the region are under cultivation, there are many places in East Anglia where the naturalist will find trees and smaller plants to interest him. Even lichens, plants that are so evident and abundant in the wetter conditions of western Britain, occur here, though few people bother to look for them.

Unmanaged woodland is very scarce indeed in East Anglia, where many plantations have been created solely as potential sources of timber, and where the interests of game preservation often lead to woods being adapted in various ways and to the exclusion of the public. Nevertheless there are stretches of woodland to which naturalists are, or may be, granted access.

Alder
    Alderwoods form a particularly interesting feature of Broadland where they are known as carrs (Icelandic *kjarr*, a fen wood). There are some fine examples in the Bure Marshes National Nature Reserve, some 1019 acres of unreclaimed fenland and broads on either side of the river Bure between Wroxham and Ranworth. Accessible only by boat, the Hoveton Great Broad Nature Trail is situated in this reserve. Starting and ending on the north bank of the River Bure at a point upstream from the entrance to Salhouse Broad, it takes the visitor through some virtually untouched alder woodland whose 'maiden' trees have single trunks (elsewhere one sees alders with several trunks, a sign that some time ago they were cut back to obtain the damp-resistant timber).

The alder, whose leaves bear red 'bead-galls' caused by microscopic mites, produces small float-bearing seeds which are well dispersed by water but less effectively by wind. Besides enabling alders to reproduce themselves, these seeds serve as food for siskins and lesser redpolls in winter.

Broadland alderwoods often contain ash trees. Their waterlogged soil also supports several shrubs, including grey sallow, buckthorn, alder buckthorn, wild black currant and guelder rose. The white flowers of the last-named species give way to clusters of brilliant red berries, winter food for waxwings, fieldfares and redwings. Climbing into the moist air of alderwoods one finds great bindweed whose large white bell-shaped flowers are visited by hawk-moths searching for nectar secreted by the base of the ovary. Wild hop also grows here, its tough stems always twining to the right (clockwise), and so does the straggling bitter-sweet or woody nightshade.

Such herbaceous plants as meadowsweet and yellow flag grow in the damp shady conditions of alderwoods but often without flowering. The stinging nettles seen here are usually of a non-stinging variety with elongated leaves. Royal fern, its spore-bearing structures (sporangia) on the upper part of the leaf (most ferns bear them on the under surface) is occasionally found in these alderwoods, but fen fern is more abundant

Left Yellow flag, a
beautiful wild iris,
which often fails to
flower in shady
Broadland
alderwoods.

Right Common
twayblade, a common
and widespread wild
orchid.

there. Of the sedges, tussock sedge (also called great stooled and great
panicled sedge) is a particularly interesting species. Its great stools, once
used as seats in cottages and as hassocks in churches, often serve as foot-
holds for young alders and sallows. The flora of alderwoods is increased
by mosses, liverworts, lichens and fungi, all thriving on trees, shrubs
and decaying trunks and branches.

Beyond the bounds of Broadland the naturalist will see alders growing
beside lakes and streams and on badly drained, low-lying land. He may
even find members of Conservation Corps removing alder saplings (and
not only this species). At Hockham Fen, Norfolk, this was done to retain
the open fen area and, as a result, the yellow flag, a beautiful wild iris,
received plenty of light and was thus able to produce its large bright
yellow flowers in abundance.

Ash, too, sometimes colonises East Anglian fens. Common in woods
and hedges in large parts of the region, it makes a tall handsome tree
when allowed to develop naturally on fertile, moist (but well drained)
soils. In this region, ash produces plenty of seeds in some years but few
or none in others. Many of the seeds left by bullfinches – to which they
are an important winter food – mice and voles succeed in germinating.
But large numbers of ash seedlings die from damping-off in damp sites,
and many others perish during winter in Breckland woods and other
dry places.

Ash

Saplings and mature trees of ash are the habitat of several gall midges
and other insects and at least two species of gall mites, one of which
converts the flower clusters into 'cauliflower' galls whose dark masses
are conspicuous on the trees in winter. In damp woods in Broadland
ash trunks are often well covered by large leafy *Parmelia* species and
several smaller lichens. Those who are more interested in wild flowers
will find many under ash trees whose open foliage allows plenty of light
to reach the ground. Dog's mercury, lesser celandine, moschatel (also

Beech

called 'town-hall clock' because four of the flowers of each cluster face in different directions), and other species thrive there.

Like ash, beech does not produce seed or 'mast' in quantity each year, 'mast' years with heavy yields often occurring at intervals of several years. Nevertheless many creatures exploit these irregular crops in East Anglia where beeches occur as isolated trees or in comparatively small plantations or 'belts' (as in Breckland). Bramblings, winter visitors from the Continent, have a great liking for beech-mast, often feeding directly from the trees, sometimes hovering to reach seeds. Chaffinches, too, are fond of beech-mast. Other birds that may be seen eating beech-mast include pheasants, woodpigeons and great spotted woodpeckers and such smaller species as nuthatches, coal and marsh tits. Squirrels enjoy beech-mast and so do those folk who have patience enough to 'shell' the oil-rich seeds.

The dense shade cast by beeches prevents most wild flowers from growing under them, but several interesting species are adapted to living in such conditions. Some of them are saprophytes, plants which, lacking the chlorophyll found in normal green plants, are unable to make sugars and proteins but have to obtain food already manufactured. Examples are the numerous toadstools growing under beeches (and in many other places): they derive food from decaying leaves, wood, manure and other matter. Yet another example is the rare bird's-nest orchid, a species of dense shade whose irregular root mass somewhat resembles an untidy bird's nest. These roots are strongly infected with a mycorhizal fungus, through which the orchid, with its tall dense spike of pale brown flowers, obtains its food from decaying leaves.

Recorded from Suffolk as early as 1562, the broad-leaved helleborine, though rare, is still found in East Anglia. It occurs under beeches and in a variety of other situations, both light and shady. Bearing slender spikes of small green flowers, the common twayblade also grows under beeches and in many other sorts of places in the region. Certain other orchids and wild flowers are found under beeches, but often the ground beneath them is carpeted only by mosses or dead leaves. On occasion exposed roots of beech trees bear a lichen, *Xanthoria parietina*, which is greyish or greenish in shade but bright orange in the open.

At Felbrigg Hall, two miles south-west of Cromer on the Norfolk coast, the National Trust has opened a woodland walk through the Great Wood where magnificent beeches may be seen. Earlier in their lives these trees were regularly cut over at a height of eight to ten feet. This pollarding resulted in the regeneration of the trunks and thus the production of a constant supply of firewood. The largest of the Felbrigg beeches are now about 100 feet high and the oldest are perhaps over 300 years old. Typical of their species, these Norfolk beeches display natural

Sand or sea pansy. This attractive species is generally regarded as a rather rare plant of coastal sand-dunes, but in East Anglia it grows inland on the Breckland sands.

Birches at South
Wootton, Norfolk.
Here, as elsewhere,
these 'ladies of the
woods' act as
invading pioneers.

beauty throughout the year: the young leaves a delicate, almost golden, green, the mature ones a shining deep green and finally a russet-brown or warm orange.

Birches

The beech is 'mother of the forest' because its leaf-litter brings fertility to the soil. But the birch is 'lady of the woods', a designation acknowledging its fragile grace, though hardly seeming to suit its role as an invading pioneer. Carried by the wind, its tiny winged seeds – a favourite food of redpolls – take the species to heaths, bare ground, gaps in woods and plantations, even the tops of old walls. Foresters and members of Conservation Corps must often remove it, just as gardeners treat weeds – 'matter in the wrong place'.

So far I have referred to 'the' birch, but two species, both common, are found in East Anglia and intermediates occur where they grow together. *Betula pendula*, the true silver or warty birch, grows in woods on light dry soils and invades heaths where it is not checked by burning, grazing, or the activities of conservationists. More tolerant of wet and cold, *Betula pubescens*, the white or hairy birch, occurs in wet woods and carr and on heaths.

Light-demanding, these birches grow rapidly, but, casting light shade, allow certain smaller plants to grow beneath them. Bluebells, red campion, germander speedwell and grasses may be among those that do so in some places. Elsewhere there may be little other than bracken. At Dunwich Heath, on the Suffolk coast, visitors following the boundary walk pass through an area of birchwood. The work of retaining the character of this National Trust property, primarily an expanse of heathland on sandy soil, includes the removal of invading birch saplings and bracken.

Two conspicuous fungi are associated with birch in East Anglia. The
fly agaric, a toadstool whose red cap is flecked with white, engages in a
co-operative partnership with the birch. Its fungal threads combine
with the tree's roots, thus promoting one another's nutrition. The other,
the birch polypore or razor-strop fungus, starts as a roundish white
knob on a branch or trunk and expands to a bracket, pale brown above
and white below. Causing a reddish rot in the sapwood, it kills many
birches. But it's an ill-wind that blows no man good: the fine powder to
which the fungus reduces the timber is used as a polishing medium by
Swiss watch-makers.

Pines

Like birches, pines (so often called 'firs') are active invaders of commons, heaths and waste land, their winged seeds being carried by wind
to places far from the parent trees. Where there is little or no grazing
and where fire – that good servant but bad master – is avoided, young
pines must be uprooted if open spaces are not to become pinewoods.
Already this problem has had to be faced at several East Anglian nature
reserves. Thetford Heath National Nature Reserve is one such place.
When acquired by the Norfolk Naturalists Trust in 1949, it was an area
of well grazed grassland and sandy lichen heath where grazing rabbits
controlled the growth of heather and many other plants, and where such
birds of the open heath as the stone curlew, wheatear and woodlark bred.
Then myxomatosis, by destroying most of the rabbits, removed a force
that had controlled not only small plants but Scots pine, hawthorn and
other woody species. Loss of suitable nesting habitat followed and, for
this and probably other reasons, heathland birds declined as breeding
species. In an effort to encourage stone curlews and other birds to breed
and to give small plants a chance, large numbers of regenerating pines
have since been pulled up and several small plots rotavated early in the

year. Then, in 1971, a flock of Welsh Border sheep was introduced as a further means of arresting the change from heath to scrub.

But there was to be no easy solution, for the sheep avoided the self-sown pine seedlings, leaving them to be cleared by voluntary workers, selected the more nutritious grasses, and grazed plants of the Breckland mugwort in an enclosure which had been damaged by trespassers.

Since the 1920s the Forestry Commission has established large pine-woods in Breckland and several other parts of East Anglia. Thetford Forest, the largest in England, alone now covers eighty-three square miles, its Scots and Corsican pines yielding a substantial harvest of timber for industry.

While it is true that many smaller plants are excluded by the dense shade created by the trees and the deep litter of needles on the ground, these pinewoods are nevertheless not without interest to botanists (and, indeed, other naturalists too). Forest rides, firebreaks, woodland margins and roadside verges are all worth examining for their wild flowers, mosses and lichens (particularly the 'reindeer mosses', 'pyxie cups' and other members of the genus *Cladonia*).

Walking along a ride through the pinewoods at Weeting one recent summer's afternoon, I found many plants in flower. There were lady's bedstraw, bird's-foot trefoil, ragwort (its leaves bearing yellow-and-black caterpillars of the cinnabar moth), greater knapweed, biting stone-crop, with bright yellow flowers, and many more. A roe deer resting in coarse vegetation beside the track bounded into the wood, pausing briefly to look at us, and further on we watched a partridge lead her chicks to safety!

Fungi abound in these East Anglian pinewoods. One of them, *Fomes annosus*, a destructive parasite of conifers, forms a bracket-shaped fruit-body, bright reddish-brown above with a hard crust and white below and at the edge. Gaining entry through the stumps of felled trees, it grows down through the root system, passing into the roots of living trees and eventually killing them. Nowadays foresters control *Fomes* by introducing into the dead stump another fungus, *Peniophora gigantea*. This species, which is not a tree killer, forms an irregular waxy crust, looking like candle grease when moist, and keeps out the harmful *Fomes*.

Critics of the Forestry Commission would do well to remember the trouble it takes to safeguard rare plants. In one of its East Anglian conifer plantations the Commission has created a reserve for the very rare soldier or military orchid. High fenced and padlocked, it is open under supervision on one or two days a year.

Long before the Forestry Commission came into being in 1919, private landowners had established pines in East Anglia. From about 1850 onwards the Coke family planted sand dunes on the north Norfolk

Bluebells flowering in an oakwood. Bracken is growing among those in the foreground.

Oaks

coast with Corsican pines to stablize them against wind erosion and to protect the reclaimed freshwater marshes (once salt marsh) from blown sand. Now included in the Holkham National Nature Reserve, these dunes display very good examples of natural regeneration by Corsican pine. Before anyone objects that these coastal pinewoods lack interest for botanists, let me recall that, during a recent October, members of the Norfolk and Norwich Naturalists' Society found about sixty species of fungi amongst the dunes and under the pines at Holkham Gap!

The Corsican pine, a Mediterranean tree, was introduced to Britain in 1759, but there are those who would include it in 'the dark alien masses,' as some people regard all conifers.

The pedunculate and sessile oaks, on the other hand, are held up as symbols of sturdiness, independence and the will to survive. That they themselves endure is evident from the number of large, stag-headed oaks still living. The Norfolk Naturalists Trust reserve at Thursford Woods, beside the Holt-Fakenham road, includes a number of ancient specimens. Saved from the timber merchant's axe many years ago by the late Edward Anderson, they stand as living monuments to three members of a family who loved the place and were buried there.

Besides oak, these woods contain ash, beech, birch, holly, bird cherry and hazel. There are larch, spruce and yew, too, all planted by the Andersons in gaps left by the timber merchant, and masses of rhododendrons. The bluebells blooming there in early summer have manufactured food in their leaves, and stored it in bulbs several inches beneath the surface of the woodland floor, before the bracken grows up and casts its shade. These wild hyacinths – to use the bluebell's other name – also produce shiny black seeds. A second means of ensuring the survival of the species, they fall from the seed capsules before the leaves wither in June. Dog's mercury also grows here, bearing its small green flowers in March and April (sometimes even earlier), but, unlike the bluebell, keeping its leaves during summer.

Naturalists will find oaks in many other parts of East Anglia. Blickling Hall, Norfolk, is one such place. Here the National Trust is replanting the woods and park, and over 1,000 oak trees were planted out of a total of about 3,500 trees of many types in 1973. In West Suffolk, Clare Castle Country Park contains young oaks and several other kinds of trees.

Insect galls are common on East Anglian oaks. Rose-pink and spongy when mature in June or July, oak apples are conspicuous and attractive galls. In summer winged males and females of the bisexual generation of the gall-wasp *Biorhiza pallida* escape from the oak apples through tiny exit holes. After mating in July the females penetrate the soil around the oak, insert their eggs in rootlets, on which spherical brownish galls develop. At the end of the second winter adult gall-wasps, the unisexual generation of *B. pallida*, leave the root-galls. These insects, all wingless virgin females, climb up the oak trunk and lay unfertilised eggs in the leaf buds where fresh oak apples form.

Oak apple galls are often confused with oak marbles, round hard galls of another gall-wasp, *Andricus kollari*. Besides these common and widespread galls, East Anglian oaks also bear spangle-galls and cherry galls on leaves, currant galls on young leaves and male catkins, and several more.

This is not the place to list the numerous other insects or, for that matter, the many species of birds associated with oaks in the region. But we must mention that in East Anglia mistletoe, a partial parasite of woodland and orchard trees, has been recorded on oak, a species less often attacked here than cultivated apples, hawthorn and poplar. Passing its entire life cycle in the tree-tops, without direct contact with the ground, this evergreen plant draws water and mineral salts from its host tree, making carbohydrates in its own green leaves.

Limes

Also acting as hosts of mistletoe, lime trees produce sweet-scented flowers whose abundant nectar attracts honeybees and bumblebees in large numbers. Aphids suck the sweet sap from lime leaves and secrete honeydew, a sugary waste product. This is infected by sooty moulds whose blackness disfigures leaves, pavements and parked cars on to which honey-dew has dripped. When nectar is not available, bees collect the sooty honey-dew but this darkens their honey.

Now naturalised here, the common lime is widespread and frequent in the region. It is a hybrid between the large-leaved and small-leaved limes, both members of the East Anglian flora. At Santon Downham, Suffolk, there is an avenue of limes where one can see some of the original common limes planted by the Downham Estate in 1880. These old trees have been in declining health for some years, and since 1947 the Forestry Commission has been felling a section of the avenue and replacing it with new trees every ten years. The replacement species, the Crimea lime

Groton Wood, Suffolk, where a fine stand of coppiced small-leaved lime occurs.

(*Tilia euchlora*), a hybrid between small-leaved lime and *Tilia dasystyla*, a rare Crimean species, does not throw up as many root-suckers as common lime and it is free from aphids.

A fine stand of coppiced small-leaved lime is to be seen in Groton Wood, a property of the Suffolk Trust for Nature Conservation, two miles north-east of Boxford. The northern part of this 50-acre reserve formed part of the manorial wood of medieval Groton. Apart from woodruff, wood spurge and wood millet, whose presence is said to suggest a continuity with medieval woodland, the naturalist will find ancient boundary banks and other earthworks.

Coppice

The old-established practice of coppicing involves cutting trees and shrubs to the ground every seven to twenty-odd years (depending on species). This encourages the production of shoots from the stumps or stools. It also brings about variations in the amount of light reaching the ground. The access of light after coppicing stimulates woodland plants to active growth and flowering. But as the coppice shoots grow up again the amount of light falling on the woodland floor is reduced, and growth and flowering of the woodland plants becomes less vigorous. This situation was reached at Bulls Wood, Cockfield, Suffolk, a 29 acre reserve jointly managed by the Forestry Commission and the Suffolk Trust for Nature Conservation. Comprising mixed general coppice and coppice-with-standards (the standards being trees that have been left to grow naturally), this wood contains mainly hazel and ash with some field maple and oak. The oxlip, a species growing in Britain in certain woods and damp meadows in the area where Suffolk, Essex and Cambridge meet, occurs throughout Bulls Wood. In recent years very few had been

Primroses flowering
beneath coppiced ash
whose leaves have yet
to unfold.

flowering there owing to the dense shade, but the plan to cut rides and
to coppice hazel and ash should result in improved conditions for the
species. With their deep yellow, primrose-like flowers in many-flowered
umbels, oxlips make a splendid display in April. But one hastens to add
that in a Cambridgeshire wood fallow deer have found these flowers to
be very palatable!

Bulls Wood is also the habitat of the little spindle tree whose deep pink
fruit open to reveal bright orange seed coverings. Like so many species
of apparent insignificance, it plays its part in nature, serving as winter
host to the bean or black aphis, a common and widespread pest of beans
and many other plants, both cultivated and wild. In this reserve, too,
spurge laurel, a shrub with evergreen leaves, bears green flowers in spring,
when another shrub, the Rocky Mountain or Oregon grape, a native of
western North America, produces clusters of yellow flowers. This last-
named species is a host of *Puccinia graminis*, a rust fungus that causes
black rust of wheat and certain other cereals, an intensively studied plant
disease. Other plants of Bulls Wood include the early purple orchid, with
spikes of reddish-purple flowers, and the distinctive herb Paris, a very
local plant whose flowers have a foetid odour attractive to carrion flies.

At Bradfield Woods Nature Reserve, a Suffolk property of the Society for the Promotion of Nature Reserves, the continuity of coppice management over the past 700 years has encouraged the growth of many different plants. One of the chief objectives of those responsible for this reserve is to continue coppice management with help from craftsmen who use materials cut there to make rakes, mallets and beetles, scythe handles, fencing stakes and other useful articles. On one edge of the wood there is birch-oak coppice where bluebells and primroses flower. In a wetter part of the wood ash-elm coppice provides a habitat for oxlips. Other areas of interest include the central birch-bracken woodland and a number of well-managed rides and ponds.

Osier and willows

The reader who has followed me up to this point will have noticed that there are many trees about which I have so far said little or nothing. The grey sallow has been mentioned but not its fellow members of the genus *Salix*, the osiers and willows. Since the time of Sir J. E. Smith, the distinguished 19th century Norfolk botanist and student of willows, the readiness with which these trees hybridise and thus puzzle botanists has been recognised.

Abundant and widespread, the common osier has frequently been planted, its long pliant shoots being used in basket-making. White willows, common and fairly large trees of damp places, have been pollarded (cut down to a height of about 6 feet), to stimulate them to throw up rods resembling osiers. They are seen lining banks of dykes and streams, their short erect trunks surmounted by heads of slender shoots. These pollard willows often support a flora of their own, brambles, elders and smaller plants growing from the layers of dead leaves trapped in their tops. The almond-leaved and purple willows grow in Broadland and other parts of East Anglia, the purple willow being used to form extensive windbreaks in the peatland of Methwold Fen.

A common tall shrub or bushy tree in woods, copses, hedges and waste places, the goat willow may be regarded as useless and worthless by foresters, but the catkins of this species are a valued source of nectar and pollen for honeybees early in the year. Bumblebees, too, visit the catkins in spring when lack of forage prevents the establishment of many colonies of these useful insects. This fact led one worker to suggest that early-flowering willows should be planted near crops requiring pollination by bumblebees.

Elms

As is the case with willows, certain species of elm are often confused with one another. This does not alter the fact that elms are an attractive feature of many East Anglian woods and hedges and that, like willows, they are useful early sources of pollen for honeybees. Wych elms have grown to impressive sizes in the region, one having attained a girth of 25 feet at Monks Eleigh, Suffolk. In that county too one finds fine examples of the English elm, which also occurs in Norfolk. Often confused with the English elm, the smooth elm is fairly common in East Anglia. One can either regard it as a single very variable species or attempt to decide whether individual 'smooth elms' belong to Melville's East Anglian elm, his Coritanian elm, or to other 'species' within the smooth elm aggregate!

Scrub

Certain of the species already mentioned occur in scrub, woody vegetation consisting entirely or mainly of shrubs. Some areas of scrub would normally progress to woodland, others, such as dense shady masses of hawthorn, gorse and blackthorn, would resist this change, at least for a time. But nowadays bulldozers and other mechanical aids make the removal of scrub a quick and easy task, and one which is often seen as a vital duty in East Anglia and other areas of intensive cultivation. Even the conservation of habitats, always something of an exercise in the art of compromise, may, as we have already seen, involve the control of scrub and even trees.

However, the importance of scrub as a valuable supplement to the larger nature reserves has been recognised. In 1972 the Tenth Triennial Conference of the Association of Parish Councils supported a resolution that the 'Year of the Tree' campaign should include the provision or acquisition of village thickets in each parish. As sanctuaries for wild life, they would be wardened by thicket keepers who would take appropriate action if rabbits, or any other species, became a nuisance. Let us hope that something comes from this initiative. Otherwise we may become *too* tidy-minded and bulldoze even more wild life out of existence.

Hedgerows

Artificial forms of scrub (as that eminent ecologist, Sir Arthur Tansley, once called them), planted hedgerows are disappearing in many parts of East Anglia as fields are enlarged and old roads widened or new ones thrown across the countryside. Hedgerow trees are also being removed in large numbers, healthy ones for their timber, others because they are dead or dying. Hedgerow trees, farmers explain, harbour pigeons and damage farm implements (which, in their turn, may damage tree roots when ploughing is undertaken close to hedges).

Hawthorn is a common East Anglian hedge shrub, but on its own, particularly when kept short and closely trimmed, it forms a hedge that, lacking variety, makes a poor habitat for wildlife. The ideal type of hedge appears to be one that is over six feet high and contains several different species of trees and shrubs, but which is not managed too frequently.

Trees present in East Anglian hedges include ash, beech, elm, oak and willow, all already referred to in this chapter. Crab apple trees, whose fruit are taken in winter by blackbirds, thrushes, waxwings, and even blue tits, occur there, as do hollies, their scarlet berries being a favourite food of mistle thrushes, pigeons and redwings (and at least six other kinds of birds), mainly in December and January. Elder, like hawthorn,

Hedgerow and scrub along Peddars Way at Massingham Heath, Norfolk.

can form a small tree, and both species produce berries that attract hungry birds. One survey recorded 32 bird species feeding on elder berries and 23 on hawthorn berries. Field maple and sycamore are also seen as hedgerow trees. Their fruits are unattractive but nevertheless find favour with mice and hawfinches. All these trees nourish numerous insect visitors in one way or another. Even tough prickly holly leaves bear patterns made by larvae of leaf-mining insects feeding inside them.

The shrubs of our hedges include the spiny blackthorn whose blue-black sloes are sour and astringent and largely ignored by birds, though hawfinches can open the stones. Privet is another, its shiny black fruits being taken by at least three bird species. Hazel, its lamb's-tail catkins an early source of pollen for bees, yields nuts that are often taken by nut-hatches, great tits and squirrels before ripening is complete. The patient searcher will find many more trees and shrubs in East Anglian hedges: red-stemmed dogwood, hornbeam grown to form windbreaks in Breck-land where isolated trees of this species attract hawfinches, and, in hedges at Hargham, Norfolk, the cornelian cherry, a native of southern Europe and western Asia, whose small yellow flowers appear before the leaves in February or March – to mention but a few.

Then there are the hedgerow scramblers, sprawlers, climbers and clingers! Scrambling through and sprawling over many of our hedges, wild roses bear red-tinted bedeguar galls (the so-called robin's pin-cushions), smooth and spiny pea-galls, curious growths caused by gall-wasps. Rose fruits, the colourful hips, provide vitamin C for those who drink rose-hip syrup and winter food for thrushes.

Honeysuckle climbs by entwining shrubs and trees with its stems. Its flowers exhale a delicious sweet scent, faint during the day, strong at night. After pollination by nectar-eating hawk-moths and, to a lesser extent, pollen-eating hover flies, they give rise to clusters of red berries which are enjoyed by birds.

White bryony clings to hedgerow shrubs by means of spiral tendrils, the greenish flowers being followed by dull red berries. Black bryony, with glossy dark green leaves, grows over hedges, its slender stems twining to the left. The small flowers are yellowish-green. The red berries, like the yellowing leaves, bring autumn colour to the hedges. Bryony berries are poisonous to us, but those of black bryony are eaten by thrushes and chaffinches after their content of poisonous saponin has been reduced by exposure to the weather.

Verges

Alongside many roadside hedgerows, as with fencing that has replaced so many of them, are verges, 'the last really big nature reserve we have in Britain except for the wild moors and lakes of our northern mountains and the seas around us' – as Charles Elton described these associated habitats. The vital role of roadside verges is evident from the fact that they form the only known habitat of seven of the rarest British plants and the main habitat of another twenty such species. Their importance is recognised in East Anglia where, as a result of co-operation between highways authorities, County Trusts, and other bodies, marker posts, usually carrying the letters NR, are being erected at suitable roadside sites which are then cut according to an agreed regime. Among the plants being conserved in this way are bee, pyramidal and early purple orchids, crested cow wheat, and Spanish catchfly, foodplant of the viper's bugloss moth, an insect whose only known British habitat is on a Suffolk road-side (Incidentally, this moth has no connection with the beautiful blue-flowered herb after which it is named).

Roadside verges are, of course, habitats of many other plants and insects, though some may be more abundant along minor roads. Germander speedwell is at home there, its deep sky-blue flowers bearing white 'eyes' and deeper blue lines, its terminal leaves commonly galled by a midge. Banished from cornfield to waste ground and roadside, common poppies colour freshly disturbed verges and banks with rich scarlet flowers (1974 was a wonderful year for them in the Bury St Edmunds area!) Both with golden yellow flowers and wind-dispersed seeds, colts-foot, which is quick to colonise disturbed ground, and dandelion are common verge plants. Coltsfoot, one of the earliest spring flowers is a useful pollen plant for bees, while dandelions provide these insects with nectar and pollen. Violet-flowered ground ivy, its leaves often bearing 'lighthouse' galls of a gall midge or the larger globular galls of a wasp, is another familiar roadside herb. Then there are the pleasantly aromatic herbs yarrow, with white or pink flowers, and mugwort, and many other plants, including several grasses, each interesting in its own particular way.

Grassland

In addition to road verges, often regarded as modified grassland, East Anglia includes areas of grassland of outstanding interest to naturalists. Mickfield Meadow, in Suffolk, an undrained reserve of 4.6 acres, was acquired by the Society for the Promotion of Nature Reserves for the conservation of snake's head fritillaries whose drooping bell-shaped flowers are dull purple and spotted, rarely white or yellowish. The meadow is damp enough for this species, but pigeons and pheasants have done considerable damage to the flowers. Other plants growing on damper areas of this reserve include meadowsweet, with creamy white flowers, wild angelica, mauve-flowered great willow herb (codlins-and-cream) and pepper saxifrage with yellow flowers. On drier areas the dominant species is meadow foxtail, a coarse tall grass.

Agreements with the owners of several other areas have been nego-tiated by the Suffolk Trust for Nature Conservation whose Conservation Officer should be consulted by naturalists wishing to see these reserves. One agreement concerns three permanent pastures. These are not under-drained and have long been managed for hay in the traditional manner, being cut late for bulk in mid-July. The dominant grass is meadow brome, but sweet vernal grass – strongly scented with coumarin, the highly palatable yellow or golden oat-grass, soft brome (also called lop grass), and common quaking-grass, a beautiful plant with drooping spikelets, also occur. Autumn crocus is abundant here, its pale purple or deep mauve flowers appearing in early September, its leaves and fruits in late spring, a situation explaining its other name, naked ladies. Snake's head fritil-laries grow here, as do cowslips, common corn rattle (also called hay rattle, a more appropriate name here), and green winged orchid. The flowers of the last-named vary in colour from deep red-purple to pale purple, lilac, pink or occasionally white. They are visited by bees which collect sugar from the fleshy walls of the spur.

An agreement with the owners of three other small pieces of old un-ploughed grassland has secured the protection of lady's mantle at one of its two East Anglian sites. With small clusters of greenish-yellow

Flowers of the snake's head fritillary at Mickfield Meadow, the Suffolk reserve devoted to the conservation of this species.

flowers on slender stalks, lady's mantle is attractive in its own quiet way. It usually produces 'bad' pollen, but sets seed without fertilisation. Cattle graze the meadows from mid-May. But, unlike pigs, which enjoy the plant's parsnip-flavoured roots, they do not appear to harm the lady's mantle.

The scarcity of typical chalk grassland in East Anglia emphasises the vital importance of the agreement by which the Norfolk Naturalists Trust secured Ringstead Downs, the largest area of such habitat in Norfolk. At this dry valley in the Middle Chalk, steep slopes rise from the sides of a flat floor. Hawthorn had spread on the slopes but already a large area of it has been cleared to encourage the growth of smaller plants. The typical chalk plants of this new reserve include yellow rock rose, a low spreading shrublet with golden flowers, squinancy wort, its pale pink-lilac flowers attracting small insects, and salad burnet, a pretty plant with greenish-purple flower-heads. Wild thyme grows there and so does an eyebright whose scientific name, *Euphrasia pseudokerneri*, has yet to give rise to an English equivalent. Stemless thistle, a single crimson-purple flower-head in the centre of its prickly leaf rosette, is another Ringstead plant, as is the bee orchid whose flowers, though normally self-pollinated, are said to be mistaken by male bees for females of their own kind.

A few scattered pieces of another type of grassland, grass heath, have survived in Breckland where farming and forestry have claimed so much of this once-widespread habitat. Half of the original 2,000 acres of Lakenheath Warren is an airfield, but the remainder escaped afforestation earlier this century because of the opposition of the commoners. Once a grazing ground for thousands of sheep and rabbits, it has, since myxomatosis, been colonised by pines, especially on the calcareous soils. In the absence of grazing animals, it is inevitable that the invasion of these grass heaths by trees, heather and other plants should be more marked. Readers will recall the methods used to control these colonisers at Thetford Heath National Nature Reserve (See p. 34). Similar work has been undertaken at Weeting Heath National Nature Reserve where bracken and coarse vegetation have been suppressed. Here, too, an enclosure to retain wild rabbits has been constructed on part of the reserve. At Weeting careful attention is being given to the conservation of spiked speedwell and other rare Breckland plants. But it is important to remember that the chief species of the different types of grass heath are the very hardy, drought resistant sheep's fescue and two other grasses – common bent (or brown top) and brown bent. 'Reindeer mosses' and other lichens of the genus *Cladonia* often form a 'mat' over parts of these heaths, absorbing moisture when it is available, becoming dry and brittle in hot weather.

Grass heath

Air view of Weeting Heath in Breckland. The conspicuous 'stone-stripes', which are picked out by the vegetation, were produced when the area was undergoing peri-glacial conditions. Part of the extensive afforestation of the surrounding country is also seen.

Heath

Lichens of the genus *Cladonia* and certain mosses are also found on East Anglian heaths whose vegetation is dominated by the common heather or ling. This small shrublet has pink, very rarely white, flowers whose nectar makes it a very valuable bee-plant. The Domesday record refers to bee-keeping in the Sandlings region along the east Suffolk coast. Formerly this was an almost unbroken strip of heathland, but most of the area has now been reclaimed for agriculture, or used for forestry, golf courses, defence purposes, urban development, or sand and gravel working. Fortunately all is not lost in this Sandlings region, for areas of heathland are conserved at Westleton Heath National Nature Reserve, within the adjoining Minsmere reserve of the Royal Society for the Protection of Birds, and at Dunwich Heath (See p. 33). Until the 1930s sheep were grazed on these heaths in spring and autumn and until the outbreak of myxomatosis in 1954 large numbers of rabbits were active there. These grazing animals largely prevented the development of scrub. After their disappearance heather and gorse grew apace and tree seedlings and bracken appeared.

In 1956, when the Nature Conservancy declared the area as a National Nature Reserve, the heather at Westleton Heath was old and did not appear to be regenerating. Bracken and birch scrub had already replaced some that had died. In order to discover whether these methods could be used to manage the heath, experimental mowing and burning were carried out. These treatments produced fresh heather growth without encouraging bracken to make any significant advances in the test areas.

As a result, areas of the reserve are to be burnt in a 5, 10 or 20 year rotation in the hope that the most suitable period will be discovered.

At Westleton Heath common heather grows in company with cross-leaved heath, with rose-coloured flowers and leaves in whorls of four, and bell heather with deep purple flowers and leaves usually three in a whorl. Common gorse, considered to be an invader rather than a true member of the heath community, occurs here, too, its yellow flowers making a glorious show in spring. Gorse recovers after heath fires by sprouting from the stumps. Resistant to heat, its hard brown seeds are distributed along footpaths by ants. A particularly interesting member of the Westleton heathland flora is common dodder. This parasite twines its slender reddish stems around heather or gorse, attaching itself by suckers through which nourishment is absorbed from the host-plant.

In Norfolk, ling heaths are found on glacial gravels behind Salthouse and Kelling and elsewhere. They also occur on the poor acid soils of the greensand ridge at such places as Dersingham, West Newton and Roydon.

In places one passes from heath on dry soil to bog on waterlogged acid peat. Owing to drainage operations which have taken place over the years, bog is no longer a common habitat in East Anglia. Among the surviving areas is the extensive bog at Roydon Common near King's Lynn, a property of the Norfolk Naturalists Trust. On acquiring the common, the Trust erected a pile-dam to maintain the water-level and thus ensure the survival of the bog plants (and also the fen plants).

Bog

Fourteen species of bog moss (*Sphagnum*), the most characteristic of the highly specialised plants inhabiting bog, occur in the Roydon Common bog. Some form cushions or carpets, others are free-floating or submerged in bog pools. The unchecked removal of these mosses would seriously alter the character of the habitat, and already it has been found necessary to prosecute several people for taking them from the reserve. Conspicuous with their white cottony heads when in fruit, are two cotton-grasses, the single-headed hare's-tail and the several-headed bog cotton. The beautiful orange-yellow flowers of bog asphodel, a species of open wet depressions, appear in July.

The three British species of sundew also grow here, their reddish leaves attracting small insects which are enfolded by glandular hairs, killed and digested. Two other types of insectivorous plant are found at Roydon Common, namely the common butterwort and the bladderwort. The butterwort, whose bright violet flowers appear in June and July, catches small insects with a sticky secretion on the upper surface of its pale yellowish leaves. The bladderwort, a submerged plant of peaty pools, traps and digests small water creatures in its bladders.

Cranberry creeps over bog mosses, it small pink flowers, somewhat like miniature cyclamens, giving rise to berries, mostly red, but a few of a speckled brown-red. The bog orchid grows in bog moss cushions. Its tiny yellowish-green flowers are of considerable botanical interest, the lip of the flower being at the back or top (usually it is at the apparent front or bottom of the orchid flower). The hair-like roots are infected with a fungus whose activity results in food being obtained for the bog orchid plant. Though it often sets them abundantly, the bog orchid does not rely on seeds for its reproduction, new plants developing from small bud-like structures which become detached from the leaf-tips.

Bogs, sometimes small remnants, survive elsewhere in the region. Those on East Winch common and Buxton Heath, Hevingham, both scheduled as Sites of Special Scientific Interest, are now reserves of the Norfolk Naturalists Trust.

Fen

Like the plants of bogs, the vegetation of fens forms peat layers. But, unlike that of bogs, the soil water of fens is not acid. Drainage and cultivation have turned many of the original East Anglian fens into rich farmland. But in Broadland fen still forms a stage in the natural succession from aquatic vegetation to damp wood or carr (See p. 30). Elsewhere in the region, valley fens border rivers and streams, as at Redgrave and Lopham Fen. On this Suffolk Trust for Nature Conservation reserve, at the headwaters of the River Waveney, there is abundant evidence of the effects of allowing such habitat to lie derelict and unmanaged. For shrubs and trees – sallow, alder, oak and birch – have moved into places where formerly the cutting of sedge and reed and the digging of peat prevented this development of the vegetation.

Now the Trust, with the help of a crawler and winch and voluntary helpers, is removing much of the encroaching scrub. But perhaps the greatest challenge facing the Trust at Redgrave and Lopham Fen is the water shortage, the result of a falling water table, following a succession of dry years and increases in the efficiency of land drainage and the demand for water. Not only is water essential in maintaining fen conditions, but it is vital in preventing and fighting fires such as that which swept through the reserve in March 1973, the third since 1967.

Middle Fen, one of the four main areas of the Redgrave and Lopham Fen Nature Reserve, is the habitat of a variety of plants. Parts of this area of old peat cuttings and ridges are dominated by the common reed, our tallest native grass, whose tough persistent stems and leaves are still used for thatching, and whose creeping rhizomes and stolons enable it to spread quickly into new territory. Some higher and drier places are occupied solely by the purple small-reed. Saw sedge, a stout hollow-stemmed perennial that is used as a capping material for thatched roofs, and blunt-flowered or fen rush grow in the bottom of old peat cuttings. Here, too, are marsh cinquefoil with dark purple flowers and bogbean whose flowers are pink and white, both plants with creeping rootstocks.

Purple moor-grass dominates the drier ridges between the old peat cuttings, while creamy-white-flowered meadowsweet and hemp agrimony, its flower-heads in crowded pink or reddish clusters, are conspicuous on the higher droves, the main paths.

Of the many other plants of this reserve, one must mention the marsh fern, a species well able to thrive in fen peat, even in thick sedge and under trees, the marsh helleborine and several other orchids (*Dactylorhiza* species). Sadly, the very rare fen orchid does not seem to have appeared here in recent years.

Like bogs and fens, marshes develop on waterlogged soil. But, unlike them, they do so on mineral soil from which peat is entirely, or very largely, absent. Having said that, one must admit that the vegetation of fens and marshes is, in many respects, similar.

Many so-called marshes have been greatly modified by drainage and grazing, but there are places along valleys of rivers and streams where drainage is defective and various rushes, sedges and grasses grow together with marsh marigold, whose flowers lack petals but bear large bright yellow petal-like sepals, early flowering lady's smock (or cuckoo flower), and ragged robin, its red petals deeply cut with narrow lobes. This is also the habitat of great hairy willow-herb, a tall mauve-flowered herb, water mint, meadowsweet and yellow flag.

The purplish-pink or rose-purple flower-spikes of the common marsh orchid make a fine sight on marshes where albino forms may also occur.

The River Waveney at Redgrave and Lopham Fens, a reserve of the Suffolk Trust for Nature Conservation.

Marshes

As its name suggests, the early marsh orchid begins flowering earlier than the previous species, its flowers, typically flesh pink, appearing in May. Common spotted orchid, with dense flower-spikes, varying from pale to deep lilac pink in colour, includes marshes among its habitats, and so does marsh fragrant orchid whose clove-scented, bright rose-red or magenta flowers form a very dense spike.

Freshwater margins

Some of the plants mentioned in the previous two sections grow along the margins of rivers and streams, ponds, lakes and broads, and even ditches, but many others are found there. Characteristic trees of such places are alder, sallows and willows, and black poplar. There are fine examples of the last-named by the river Lark in Breckland. In East Anglia many stretches of freshwater are fringed by swamp plants such as reeds and reedmace whose seeds germinate on exposed mud. Water betony, with liver-coloured flowers pollinated by wasps, and purple loosestrife, its three types of flower structure ensuring cross-pollination by insects, are among the taller colourful species of the waterside. Less colourful, with very pale flowers, the marsh sowthistle reaches a height of eight feet on clayey river banks in the eastern part of East Anglia. After becoming almost extinct at the end of the last century, this rare British plant has colonised considerable lengths of banks where mud dredged from rivers has been deposited.

Two 'alien' balsams have also shown themselves to be effective colonists of river banks (and other damp places) in the region. This is not perhaps surprising when one considers the explosive manner in which the seeds are scattered, the rapid growth of the seedlings, and the tendency of the mature plants to dominate smaller species. The large flowers of Himalayan balsam, also called policeman's helmet, are purple and white, while those of orange balsam, the jewel-weed of its native North America, are, as its name suggests, a warm orange. Another native of North America, the water musk or monkey-flower, its beautiful yellow flowers spotted with red, continues to increase along streamsides.

Aquatic habitats

East Anglian streams, broads, ponds, and other inland waters hold a variety of plants. Some of them may be seen without venturing off the beaten track. In the very heart of Thetford, for example, the Little Ouse is the habitat of pondweeds, duckweed and arrowhead whose flower-spikes and arrow-shaped leaves project from the water (it also produces floating and submerged leaves of other shapes). In Broadland dykes whorled spikes of light mauve flowers of water violet, a member of the primrose family, appear above the water, its finely divided leaves remaining submerged. Frogbit with rounded leaves and three-petalled white flowers float here in summer. Water soldier, once said to look rather like a floating pineapple-top, may block dykes completely. It spreads entirely by vegetative means, ripe seed being unknown in this country.

Left Flowers of marsh marigold whose bright yellow petal-like sepals compensate for the lack of petals.

Right Yellow water-lily (flowers and floating leaves) and water soldier (upright leaves) at Hickling Broad, Norfolk.

Since the early 1950s much of the once-abundant aquatic vegetation has vanished from many of the broads. At Hoveton Great Broad, part of the Bure Marshes National Nature Reserve, water soldier, water milfoil and the delicate water fern, a small introduced species whose floating 'mats' are red, have decreased considerably and may even have disappeared. But yellow and white water-lilies still occur there. With its flowers held above the water, the yellow water-lily produces ovoid fruits whose shape (rather than the scent of the flower) is believed to have given rise to its name of brandy bottle. The long-stalked flowers of the white water-lily, formerly called water roses, lie on the surface of the water.

Aquatic plant life is still abundant in Hickling Broad where the main channels are kept clear in summer by means of a special weed cutting machine. Green algae, various pondweeds, bladderworts and whorled water-milfoil are among the submerged plants of the brackish waters of this National Nature Reserve. Of particular interest there is the holly-leaved naiad, also known as stagshorn weed, a species unknown outside Broadland in this country. Also found in a number of other broads, including Upton Broad (freshwater), this rare plant forms extensive beds in water as deep as seven feet.

Despite their tendency to dry out, the Breckland meres are the habitat of shining and various-leaved pondweeds and their hybrid *Potamogeton x zizii*. Home Mere, on Thorpe Heath, West Wretham, forms the habitat of shoreweed. A very rare species in the region, it does not flower until the water-level falls and exposes the plant. On a number of occasions in the past the dry bed of Fowlmere was cultivated, but several times the water rose suddenly and the crop was left unharvested or, as in the case of beet and mangolds one year, gathered by men standing in the water.

Left Flowers of marsh marigold whose bright yellow petal-like sepals compensate for the lack of petals.

Right Yellow water-lily (flowers and floating leaves) and water soldier (upright leaves) at Hickling Broad, Norfolk.

Dune development at Blakeney Point, Norfolk, showing sand accumulating over shingle round plants of marram grass and saltwort.

Coastal plants in Breckland

Coastal dunes and slacks

Growing inland on the Breckland sands are several plants usually associated with the sea-coast. The most attractive of these is the sand or sea pansy. Generally regarded as a rather rare plant of coastal sand-dunes, it is restricted in East Anglia to Breckland where it is locally abundant at Santon. Its spurred flowers are variable in colour, being yellow, blue-violet or parti-coloured. Sand sedge, known locally as net-rein, is another plant of coastal dunes which occurs in Breckland. With a rootstock that creeps for several feet in sand, it is a useful sand-binder. But this sand stabilization has caused problems at Wangford Warren, a 38-acre reserve of the Suffolk Trust for Nature Conservation near Brandon. For the main object on these inland sand dunes is to conserve the status of one of the last remaining areas of active erosion in the Breckland, and certain parts have to be rotovated to prevent the sedge from arresting this erosion! Grey hair grass, a densely tufted perennial, also grows at Wangford Warren, one of the very few British inland sites for this rare grass of coastal sand-dunes. Sand cat's-tail and bearded fescue are two other grasses of coastal sands that occur in Breckland.

At the coast, sand couch, a species that is tolerant of salt, is a very important grass. Its extensive creeping roots bind sand, while the grass tufts themselves trap it. These factors enable sand couch to form low embryo dunes. Examples of these and later developments can be seen at several points on the East Anglian coast, notably at Blakeney Point Nature Reserve and Scolt Head National Nature Reserve.

Marram grass, which may be said to follow sand couch, plays a vital part in dune growth. The shoots grow upwards and outwards, trapping sand blown from the beach, while the roots reach great depths, holding sand in place. As the dune grows, spaces between tufts of the dominant marram are invaded by other plants. Sea sandwort, with fleshy leaves and spreading branches and roots, is one. Sea-holly, whose beautiful blue, thistle-like flowers are so attractive to butterflies and other insects, is another. Sand fescue, lyme grass and certain mosses may also be present, as may such colourful wild flowers as ragwort, biting stonecrop and bird's-foot trefoil.

After this yellow dune stage, whose name derives from the presence of patches of bare sand, comes the grey dune stage when exposed sand is covered by grasses, mosses and lichens. Marram gives way to sand sedge and sand fescue, and new plants replace sea sandwort, sea-holly and others. Among the typical plants of the grey dune phase at Scolt Head Island are ragwort, hound's tongue, whose dull purplish-red flowers smell of mice when bruised, lady's bedstraw, with yellow flowers smelling strongly of cumarin, bird's-foot trefoil, and wild lettuce. Shrubs, probably grown from seeds carried by birds, include brambles, privet and elder. Many other species occur on the older dunes from time to time, some disappearing after a while, making each visit something of a journey of discovery for even the most experienced naturalist.

The largest mainland dune system on the East Anglian coast is at Winterton Dunes National Nature Reserve, about 8 miles north of Great Yarmouth. Extending northwards from Winterton for nearly two miles, it covers an area of 259 acres. A particularly interesting member of the flora of these dunes is the rare hybrid marram grass, a natural hybrid between marram grass and the wood smallreed, parents that very rarely occur together!

Behind the dunes are shallow depressions. These dune slacks, as they are known, are of considerable interest because they are colonised by cross-leaved heath and other plants characteristic of acid soils (the sandy soils of many dunes contain shell fragments and show an alkaline reaction).

Eroded dunes – areas where most of the sand has disappeared and shingle has been exposed – are the habitat of many lichens. At Scolt Head they include several cup-lichens, 'reindeer mosses' and other species of *Cladonia*. The important larger plants of one such area at Scolt Head are rock sea-lavender, a variable species with violet-blue flowers, and shrubby seablite, a fleshy-leaved Mediterranean shrub which reaches its most northerly limit on the north Norfolk coast.

Several of the plants found on dunes are characteristic of shingle. This habitat of water-worn pebbles and stones is well represented in East Anglia. In Norfolk it is especially important at Blakeney Point, which

Shingle

Above left Sea holly, a plant of coastal dunes. Butterflies and other insects visit its beautiful blue flowers.

Above right Sea campion whose dainty white flowers enliven coastal shingle.

Below left Yellow horned poppy, a fine plant whose thick tap-root is thrust deep into coastal shingle.

Below right Sea lavender, whose beautiful flowers enliven salt marshes, stands up to severe winters but suffers badly in other ways.

is joined to the cliffs at Weybourne by a six-mile shingle bank. Another such bank stretches along the shore of the Wash from Snettisham to Wolferton. In Suffolk, Orford Ness forms one of the largest shingle spits in the country, extending southward for some 12 miles from Aldeburgh. A vast quantity of shingle from this spit was thrown up at and near Shingle Street and this has since been supplemented by material resulting from ordinary wastage of the spit.

Elsewhere along this coast, banks of shingle fringe the beaches. Dunwich is one such place and here, as on other Suffolk shingle banks, one finds the sea pea, its bright purple flowers fading to blue. This lovely plant is not native to Norfolk, but seeds have been sown at Blakeney and Cley. Sea campion, a widely distributed shingle plant, bears dainty white flowers close to the surface. Sea sandwort (already mentioned as a species of growing dunes) shares its ability to survive burial by stones by throwing up new aerial shoots. Yellow horned poppy, whose name refers to its large yellow flowers and long curved seed-pods, thrusts its thick tap-root deep into shingle. At Shingle Street it continues flowering well into October, as does yellow vetch. A much taller shingle plant is the maritime variety of the curled dock, a perennial up to four feet high, whose leaves are usually more fleshy than those of the common inland form. Herb Robert, an inland plant, mainly of woods, produces a purple-tinged maritime form with succulent narrowly-cut leaves. This grows on shingle beaches at Wolferton and Snettisham.

Shingle is the habitat of a number of lichens. The leafy *Xanthoria parietina* is bright orange, but at first sight many of the others look like dark or rusty stains on pebbles. It was found at Blakeney Point that where blown sand was likely to occur lichen cover was reduced and these plants were confined to the sides of pebbles. It was also observed that pebble size had a significant quantitative effect on the lichen flora, the minimum diameter for lichen establishment being about 1 cm.

Besides forming the habitat of plants and other living things, shingle ridges assist in the formation of salt marshes or saltings. They do so by protecting flat ground behind them from wave action, allowing sand and mud carried in by the tide to be laid down there. On the East Anglian coast there are several stretches of salt marsh where halophytes, specialised plants adapted to living under saline conditions, survive (even thrive on) a periodic covering by sea-water.

Salt marshes

There is a fine development of salt marshes behind Scolt Head Island (a barrier beach) and Blakeney Point (a spit) and along other parts of the north Norfolk coast. Here naturalists have long been able to observe the growth in height and area of mud patches on the sand flats, the arrival of halophytes, effective trappers of silt, the increase of vegetation and the formation of deep creeks, processes which leave numerous ill-drained

Sea aster, with flowers resembling Michaelmas daisies, plays an important part in the development of salt marshes by trapping silt among its tussocks.

depressions known as salt pans. Eventually the marshes reach such a height that they are only covered by occasional tides. Less silt is deposited, but the vegetation continues to change slowly. Finally comes the time when, as has happened so much along the coast of the Wash in recent years, the marsh is reclaimed and enclosed for cultivation.

The plants appearing at different stages of salt marsh development are of great interest, but here we have space for only a few. Bringing colour to a grey-green landscape, thrift or sea pink produces pink flowers from April to late summer or early autumn when the violet-blue flowers of sea lavender brighten the saltings and attract innumerable bees. Thrift, whose grass-like leaves form a cushion or rosette, belongs to the higher levels of salt marshes in certain parts of East Anglia, but on Blakeney Point it is essentially a shingle plant. Elsewhere at the coast it grows on cliffs and walls, while a hairy-stemmed, broad-leaved form ascends high into mountains. In gardens it is familiar to thousands who never visit salt marshes. And so is common sea lavender, for this beautiful plant of the middle levels of salt marshes also grows in ordinary garden soil. A perennial herb with a deep tap-root and stout woody stock, it stands up to severe winters but suffers badly from trampling and grazing, pollution and competition of taller growing species.

Sea aster, a close relation of the garden Michaelmas daisy, is an important marsh-forming plant. It grows at the lower levels of salt marshes among annual species of glasswort or marsh samphire, fleshy bright green plants that, pickled in hot vinegar, are a traditional Norfolk delicacy. The accumulation of silt among the sea aster tussocks causes the level of the marshes to increase. Sadly, in some places, the form with mauve ray florets is now much less common than the ray-less one with only the yellow disc florets.

Among the earliest colonists of bare mud, the annual glassworts (just mentioned) are being displaced from their pioneering role by cord-grass (also called rice-grass). Capable of colonising very sloppy mud, cord-grass is, in some localities, also replacing eel-grass, the three species of which are our only truly marine flowering plants. Anchored in the mud by long thick roots, cord-grass relies for 'feeding' on its branched surface roots. Its shoots collect silt and plant remains and thus, by helping to raise the level of the marsh, make it a valuable agent in stabilisation and reclamation of loose muddy foreshores. At Scolt Head small areas of cord-grass were cleared from Cockle Bight as its spread was threatening to impair the value of the feeding ground for the brent geese, wild duck and wintering waders.

Another grass that is widespread in salt marshes is common salt-marsh grass, also called sea meadow-grass. It forms a pure sward, providing good grazing on the upper levels, and remains the dominant plant for several years after the marsh has been reclaimed from the sea. A vigorous perennial, salt-marsh grass is almost, if not completely, unique in its ability to survive in competition with well established sea purslane on occasion. This shrubby plant with silvery white leaves lines the sides of creeks in the lowest marshes, but at higher levels spreads and suppresses most other plants.

Naturalists who venture on to them will find that salt marshes are the habitat of many other species. Over the years they will discover there for themselves evidence of growth and change. The results of severe storms, such as the covering of areas of salt marsh by sand and shingle, will provide examples of sudden and violent change. Indeed here, as in so many parts of East Anglia, there is no shortage of material for observation.

Birds

Scientific names of birds mentioned here are included in the *List of East Anglian Birds* (p. 138–145), where the reader will find brief notes on most species recorded for Norfolk and Suffolk, including many not mentioned in this chapter.

Sea-birds
Terns

Terns, slender, fork-tailed birds whose charm is enhanced by their graceful hovering flight are given pride of place here largely because of their emblematic association with the Norfolk Naturalists' Trust, the first, and for nearly twenty years the only, body of its kind in the country. Four species of terns – Arctic, common, little and Sandwich terns – breed in the region. Their strongholds include the reserves at Scolt Head Island, Blakeney Point and Minsmere.

At one time tern eggs were gathered for domestic use and, like the birds themselves, taken for collections. This has virtually ceased, but increasing human pressure causes terns (and other species) to desert public places and move into wardened areas. Minsmere Bird Reserve is one such place. Here 1,500 additional pairs of terns and other birds have been attracted by the construction of 'The Scrape', forty acres of shallow, brackish water with many islands.

When nesting on the ground on marshes and on sand or shingle by the sea, terns lose many eggs and young to predators, which also attack the full-grown birds. Given the chance, foxes, rats, stoats and weasels will play havoc in a ternery. Short-eared owls on their nightly visits destroy both chicks and adult terns, and egg-eating by gulls and oyster-catchers can also affect the tern population. Eggs and nestlings may be swept away by rough seas or high tides, buried by blown sand, or over-whelmed by foam. Rain and cold winds cause heavy losses of chicks,

Common tern feeding at Minsmere, one of its strongholds on the East Anglian coast.

while bad conditions prevent terns from fishing out at sea, though small fish for the young may be found in the shallow water of estuaries and harbours at low tide.

Reserve managers cannot regulate all these factors, but they can, and do, control predators. They also restrict the movements of visitors during the nesting season (early May – late July) when hundreds, or even thousands, of well camouflaged eggs and chicks are crowded into comparatively small areas. They can create facilities for the use of birds, as illustrated in my reference to 'The Scrape'. Another good example is the provision of specially constructed rafts to encourage nesting by common terns at Ranworth Broad where they started breeding regularly in 1949 when old wherries were used as nesting sites.

Gulls

Widespread and adaptable, black-headed gulls often nest in ternery areas where their success as a breeding species can create problems. They suck the eggs and kill the chicks of common and little terns, rob these and Sandwich terns of fish intended for their own young, and their growing populations make increasing demands on the space available for nesting sites. Black-headed gulls have harmed terns and avocets at Minsmere and Havergate Island, where control of gulls by egg and nest removal has been practised for several years. The Havergate colony has been reduced from 6,000 pairs (1960) to between 500 and 1,500 pairs,

Black-headed gull at Minsmere where the population of this species is controlled in the interests of certain other birds.

while that at Minsmere, which began in 1964, is controlled at between 300 and 400 pairs. Natural checks operate on these birds, as when two stoats destroyed over 80 black-headed gull nests at Scolt Head Island, but systematic gull management may well prove to be in the best interest of all species concerned.

Black-headed gulls breed inland at Alderfen Broad, Wissington and Bury Beet Factory ponds, and several other places. In 1964 they finally left the historic gullery at Scoulton Mere, where formerly thousands of eggs were collected each year for sale as 'plovers' eggs'.

Herring gulls bred in East Anglia for the first time in 1958 when two pairs nested in the avocet colony at Havergate Island, while at Minsmere, where they have also bred, these great scavengers preyed on the young of Sandwich terns and black-headed gulls. The lesser black-backed gull, an aggressive and successful predator, bred at Havergate Island in 1957 and again the following year, but further breeding seems to have been discouraged in the interests of the avocets. Herring and lesser black-backed gulls breed on the shingle of a 'closed area' at Orfordness, but these colonies are shrouded in mystery. A pair of herring gulls reared three chicks at Blakeney Point in 1972, creating the first Norfolk breeding record for this species.

The common gull has nested at Blakeney Point, Minsmere and Scolt Head, but has made little headway as a breeding species in the region. Normally nesting on sea-cliffs, kittiwakes breed on ledges on the South Pier at Lowestoft. They have built nests of seaweed and twigs on the dunes at Blakeney Point and Scolt Head Island, but either failed to lay fertile eggs or were thwarted by floods and wind-blown sand. Their attempts to colonise cliffs in north-east Norfolk also appear to have been unsuccessful.

Fulmar

The fulmar *has* spread in Norfolk since successful breeding was first proved there in 1947, though it has suffered setbacks due to cliff-falls and egg-stealing, a serious matter for this species since the single egg is not normally replaced. This magnificent glider nests on ledges in cliffs

The lapwing's decline on farmland as a breeding species has caused concern among scientists.

between Weybourne and Mundesley and at Hunstanton, leaving these sites in August and returning in November.

The *List of East Anglian Birds* (p. 138–145) includes other sea-birds seen in our coastal region. Cormorants, for example, assemble on Breydon in winter, roosting in trees at Ranworth Broad. Away from the coast black and common terns visit Breckland meres and other inland waters while in winter herring, great black-backed, common and black-headed gulls find food on refuse tips. The last two species follow the plough, taking earthworms and grubs, always ready to seize mice that may be disturbed.

Waders
Lapwing

Our most familiar wader, the lapwing, also follows the plough, often in company with gulls and starlings. Its decline on farmland as a breeding species is being investigated by scientists of Monks Wood Experimental Station. They are interested in comparing the diet and breeding performance of lapwings on arable farmland with the situation in Breckland and the river meadows of the East Anglian fens.

Stone curlew

Similar data are being collected for the stone curlew. Formerly regarded as a characteristic bird on the open Breckland heaths, the thick-knee or Willie Reeve (to use two of the stone curlew's local names) now occurs in much smaller numbers. Afforestation has taken place over much of Breckland, and in places heath has given way to scrub since myxomatosis severely reduced the rabbit population. But fortunately the stone curlew still finds nesting sites in forest rides and clearings, on cultivated land and in places where sheep keep vegetation down. This summer visitor with the shrill wild cry has long been known as the Norfolk plover, but it was left to the Suffolk Trust for Nature Conservation to adopt it as its emblem!

Ringed plover

The ringed plover was also listed as a typical bird of Breckland heaths, but it has become rare there. Nowadays it is found in numbers on the coast at Blakeney Point and Scolt Head where it is seen running along the shore, stopping to feed rapidly on insects, worms or molluscs. Ringed plovers will drive away birds much bigger than themselves, but they do

not always succeed in preventing rooks and carrion crows from robbing their more exposed nests. Nesting ringed plovers have shared a Norfolk gravel pit with the little ringed plover, a scarce species favouring pits where work is in progress. Ringed plovers harried a pair of Kentish plovers nesting near them at Walberswick in 1952. Now extinct as a British breeding species, the Kentish plover was making its only recorded attempt to breed in East Anglia.

Black-tailed godwit

1952 will also be remembered as the year a pair of black-tailed godwits colonised the Ouse Washes (Cambridgeshire/Norfolk), well over a hundred years after the species had ceased to breed regularly in the fenland. In 1973, despite dry conditions, there were at least 51 pairs there. Breeding male black-tailed godwits will make considerable efforts to defend their nesting territories, chasing away rival males, carrion crows and even birds as large as herons and Canada geese. But at the Ouse Washes, where flooding and trampling by grazing cattle have also caused breeding losses, they have not always been able to ward off predators such as carrion crows, jackdaws, rats and stoats. Similar setbacks have occurred at Cley marsh since black-tailed godwits first attempted to breed there in 1964, but it is encouraging to be able to report that two pairs bred 'somewhere in Suffolk' in 1972.

In Holland the black-tailed godwit is known as 'King of the meadow birds'. The children of Fridalen Primary School in Norway, who protested to *The Observer* about the destruction of numbers of this bird in Britain, obviously think just as highly of the oystercatcher, for they call

A snipe at Minsmere where this species can still enjoy wet feeding in muddy places. Many of its former habitats are now too dry.

this black-and-white shore-bird the Gentleman of the Shore 'because of the elegant way in which it struts around'. When oystercatchers feed on cockles and mussels in areas where they are commercially important demands do arise for their destruction, and this has happened in, for example, the Brancaster Staithe area. This is close to Scolt Head Island, the habitat of 150 breeding pairs of sea-pies (to use the local name) and on the same stretch of Norfolk coast is Blakeney Point with 120 pairs. Oystercatchers also nest inland, one pair having bred successfully at Sculthorpe aerodrome near Fakenham.

Oystercatcher

The redshank formerly nested inland on rivers, lakes and heaths, but its numbers have declined in these localities. It still breeds at Blakeney Point, Scolt Head, Welney Wildfowl Reserve, and several other places where its clear flute-like call must have led many people to echo the old marshman's words 'The place'd be dead without them birds, but they make it a paradise.' The same might well be said of the curlew when its loud wild call is heard in The Wash, on saltings and mudflats, and in Breckland, where it has bred since the end of the Second World War in open spaces between forestry plantations.

Redshank

Curlew

Breckland is one of several strongholds of breeding woodcock, a species whose increase in East Anglia is noteworthy. The only wading bird adapted to a woodland habitat, the woodcock has shown a marked preference for pine woods in parts of the region, occasionally bringing in oak leaves as a nest-lining. Nesting on the ground among dead leaves where its plumage is difficult to distinguish, the woodcock benefits from camouflage. But unfortunately this does not always safeguard it from stoats and other predators.

Woodcock

The snipe is a diminishing breeding species, drainage and cultivation of boggy ground, and dredging of rivers and drying out of adjoining meadows, having rendered much land unsuitable for a bird given to wet feeding in muddy places.

Snipe

An avocet photographed at Minsmere where the species breeds on 'The Scrape' islands.

Avocet

A completely different story can be told about the avocets of Havergate Island near Orford, for it was *neglect* of the drainage ditches and sluice, with the consequent flooding of the grazing land, which produced suitable conditions for these long-legged, black-and-white waders. Four or five pairs reared at least eight young there in 1947, over a hundred years since avocets had bred regularly in Britain. The Royal Society for the Protection of Birds, now proud to display the avocet as its official symbol, bought the island, and by 1973 the avocets had increased to 112 pairs. Black-headed gulls have harmed avocets (See p. 59), whose chicks have also been taken by kestrels and herons. Some avocet nests have been lost to carrion crows and stoats. Others have been flooded, though it has proved possible to save a number of nests by rapid manipulation of water levels. Changes in weather, high winds and falling temperature, have also caused losses of chicks. But the R.S.P.B. has never allowed these difficulties to discourage it from making every possible effort to maintain Havergate as a breeding station for avocets. Units of the Royal Engineers helped by taking bulldozers, scrapers and other equipment to the island, extending the avocets' nesting and feeding territories by creating lagoons and islands in the central part, previously an area of rough grass. They also drilled an artesian well, providing comparatively fresh water with which to 'top up' the lagoons and keep the salinity down.

Several weeks before the Havergate colony was discovered, four pairs of avocets were found nesting in a flooded field at Minsmere, another R.S.P.B. reserve, in 1947. None bred there again until 1963 when a pair nested. Since then the Minsmere avocet population has gradually increased, and in 1973 thirty-three pairs bred on The Scrape islands, sixty young having hatched by the end of June. Like those at Havergate, the Minsmere avocets have suffered from predators, including a fox which took eight clutches of eggs.

Greylag goose. Genuine wild greylags are very
scarce visitors to East Anglia, but in Broadland
there are many full-winged breeding greylags of
feral origin.

The common sandpiper, which does not breed regularly in East Anglia but has done so several times this century.

Ruff

Yet another exciting event took place in 1963 when the ruff bred on the Ouse Washes, providing the first authentic British breeding record for this species for 41 years. Seven years later, the first reeves' nests were found on the Norfolk stretch of these Washes. Annual breeding numbers for the area as a whole have fluctuated, but one cannot always be precise about them as nesting reeves are of a secretive nature and their nests are often completely hidden in thick grass. The males are quite conspicuous when sporting the ruffs and ear-tufts of their breeding finery.

Other waders

Before the reader is left to refer to the *List of East Anglian Birds* for notes on other waders seen in the region, it should be mentioned that two species which do not nest in Norfolk or Suffolk regularly have bred here this century, the common sandpiper several times inland and the dunlin twice, on grazing marshes at Salthouse on both occasions. Several of the waders not mentioned in this section are seen in East Anglia, often in large numbers, as passage migrants, winter visitors, or non-breeding summer visitors. The great estuary of Breydon Water, on the Norfolk/Suffolk boundary, is the haunt of many waders (and other species). The 22 species of waders seen there in a recent May included curlew-sandpiper, bar-tailed godwit, spotted redshank, turnstone, grey plover and knot. The Wash is an even greater haunt of waders, whose movements to roosting banks along the coast may be observed from Hunstanton cliffs at high water. Thousands of knots, bar-tailed godwits, oyster-catchers and other waders are involved in these tidal movements. The Blyth and Stour estuaries are also feeding grounds of certain waders, and the naturalist who is prepared to venture off the beaten track will discover others for himself.

Waterfowl

A truly extraordinary event was an attempt by whooper swans to breed in Norfolk in 1928, when a pair built a nest on the Merton estate. Unfortunately one bird left early in April, the other at the end of May,

Swans

A family of mute swans (male on the left), graceful birds which can cause problems for conservationists and others.

a fortnight after the nest had been found to be empty. Nowadays this species and Bewick's swan, both birds of northern open waters in Europe and Asia, are seen as passage migrants and winter visitors to the Ouse Washes, Breckland meres and some other East Anglian waters.

More familiar but no less interesting, the mute swan breeds regularly in East Anglia on inland waters and grazing marshes, and at times considerable herds may be seen on the Alde, Stour and Breydon estuaries, at Hickling, King's Lynn quays and, when flooded, the Ouse Washes. This graceful bird can be something of a problem species. Farmers object to this wasteful feeder consuming, trampling and fouling their leys and corn crops, while freshwater anglers sometimes complain of the destruction of water vegetation and of disturbance by swans. Naturalists cannot but help call attention to the way in which swans will disturb or interfere with other waterfowl. One summer a pair on Redgrave lake killed some Canada and domestic goslings and Aylesbury ducklings and drove off two pairs of great crested grebes. Difficulties have arisen for Electricity Board engineers who have re-sited certain overhead electricity lines to avoid power failures caused by swans flying into them.

Brent geese, which also winter on the Orwell and other estuaries, are recorded in varying numbers from mid-September to early May on the north Norfolk coast. Large flocks of brents, the most gregarious of all geese, may be seen there, at Blakeney-Morston, Brancaster and Wells. Studies on the feeding behaviour of brents were carried out at Scolt Head Island (Ranwell and Downing, 1959). Eel-grass or grass-wrack (*Zostera*), our only flowering plant that grows actually under the sea, was found to be an important food in autumn and early winter, marine algae (*Enteromorpha* species) the main food throughout most of the winter, and sea aster, salt-marsh grass (*Puccinellia maritima*) and other salt-marsh plants an important part of the diet in late winter. These observations supported Dr. Finn Salomonsen's suggestion (made about the same time) that ornithologists may have overestimated the dependence of brent geese on eel-grass, which was attacked on both sides of the Atlantic by a catastrophic epidemic in the thirties. Certainly brents have a more varied diet than many people realise.

Several other species of geese visit the East Anglian coast and estuaries and the Ouse Washes in winter (See *List of East Anglian Birds*). During the breeding season fewer species are represented in the region. One of them is the Canada goose. First introduced to England from North America in the 17th century, this 'black goose' has increased and spread in recent years due largely to artificial dispersion. The main British colony is at Holkham Park, Norfolk, but this goose breeds on islands in lakes and flooded gravel pits in many other places, too. Holkham Park is also the headquarters of a large full-winged colony of another introduced species, the Egyptian goose, the main domestic bird of ancient Egypt and the sacred bird of the god Geb.

There is nothing exotic about the greylag goose. Britain's only native breeding goose, it became extinct in England in the 18th century, the full-winged breeding greylags seen in Broadland today being of feral origin, the descendants of two pricked geese introduced from Scotland by Col. Cator in 1935. These Broadland greylags are well established and recently it was suggested that they and Canada geese were present at Barton Broad Reserve 'in larger numbers than is desirable,' their grazing having had quite a marked effect on some of the vegetation. Genuine wild greylags, whose clamour recalls that of grey farmyard geese, their descendants, are very scarce visitors to East Anglia nowadays.

The shelduck, the large goose-like bird of sandy and muddy shores, is abundant. In many places it formerly nested mainly in old rabbit burrows, as much as 10 ft from the surface, a habit that gave rise to the Norfolk name of burrow duck. Since myxomatosis severely reduced the

The shoveler is an East Anglian breeding duck whose food is mainly animal matter.

Spoonbills at Minsmere where courtship behaviour has been observed.

rabbit population the shelduck has often had to adapt to more open sites, nesting in dense tufts of marram grass and under bramble bushes and other ground vegetation. In Suffolk nesting in hollow trees is an old habit of this species, which also breeds in several inland localities (In 1957 shelducks nested on bombed sites in Ipswich and tried to move their young on foot through the streets!)

Many other types of duck are seen in the region, some congregating in large flocks on coastal marshes, the Broads and the Ouse Washes in winter. Thousands of mallard, wigeon, teal and other duck may then be seen feeding and in flight, but many individuals leave the area later and, in any case, some of the wintering species do not breed here at all, while others may only do so irregularly.

Scarce as a breeding species in Britain, the gadwall became established in Breckland after a pair caught in Dersingham decoy were pinioned and released on Narford lake about 1850. Their descendants multiplied and spread and East Anglia is now an important breeding area for this duck. Even less plentiful than the last bird as a British breeding species, the garganey nests at Minsmere and in Broadland. The male was dubbed cricket teal because of the curious sound it makes in the breeding season, though this has been described as being more like the grinding of teeth than the chirp of a cricket on the hearth!

Two diving ducks, pochard and tufted duck, have nested at lakes and meres in Breckland for many years, also doing so in other parts of East Anglia from time to time. They often associate with one another, but their choice of food is usually quite different. Pochard feed mainly on vegetable matter, tufted duck, locally 'black and white poker', consuming mostly animal material such as insects, molluscs and crustacea.

Another East Anglian breeding duck is the shoveler whose long bill gives it a top-heavy appearance. It nests in coarse grass or nettles, often on grazing marshes. Certain seeds are eaten, but much of this surface-feeder's food is animal matter, including small snails, crustacea, aquatic insects and their larvae.

The waterfowl collected together as 'stork and herons' include some particularly fascinating species (not that any species lacks interest for the careful and patient observer). Known in East Anglia as banjo-Bill, the spoonbill has not bred here for hundreds of years, though it still visits such places as Breydon, Cley, Hickling and Minsmere. There were two distinct pairs at Minsmere in 1970 when courtship behaviour, including carrying straws and sticks, was observed.

Spoonbill

White storks have never bred in the region and are not regular visitors. Those arriving in Norfolk in April 1967 were part of a remarkable influx of a least 13 birds in East Anglia and southeast England. Two of these storks remained all summer on Halvergate marshes near Great Yarmouth, feeding all day in dykes, roosting on old drainage mills, and giving magnificent aerial displays at great heights. In early autumn they fed on the open marshes, taking moles, shrews, short-tailed field voles and beetles. Later, during hard weather, they accepted food from roadmen, becoming almost fearless and wandering on to the road. At Christmas one stork died, apparently after colliding with overhead power cables. The other continued to be fed daily during frosty weather and remained until April 1968. It was most unusual that they did not migrate to join their species wintering in Africa. Whether storks will ever nest in East Anglia remains to be seen. White storks did rear one or two young almost annually in Kew Gardens, Surrey, between 1902 and 1916. Left unpinioned one year, the young flew away in autumn but never returned. In 1936 an attempt to establish the stork as a breeding species in England failed when storks' eggs were placed in herons' nests in Kent.

Stork

Young herons in
their nest.

Heron

The only bird of the stork kind seen regularly and commonly in Britain, the heron nests in East Anglia at some 45 sites, mostly in trees, but in reedbeds at Minsmere. Nicknamed Old Franky in Broadland, from its harsh call-note 'Frank, frank', and commonly called harnsa (or harnser), this fish-eating bird is being studied by scientists of Monks Wood Experimental Station. They state that shells of British herons' eggs are now only about four-fifths as thick as those laid over 30 years ago. This is believed to be caused by the presence of residues of certain persistent organochlorine pesticides in herons, as is almost certainly the phenomenon of these birds breaking their own eggs. As the result of coloured rings being placed on the legs of nestlings fledged there, interchange of birds between the Denver (Norfolk) colony and neighbouring ones up to 25 miles away has been observed. Herons may be seen at their traditional nesting sites from late January to August or September, but at other times they visit tidal estuaries and the seashore.

Bittern at nest with
young in East Anglia
whose large reedbeds
form the British
headquarters of this
elusive species.

Many herons died in such places during the exceptionally hard winter
of 1962–63.

Bittern

Bitterns also perished then, though some, like three half-starved ones
at Horsey, were fed and cared for by local people. Re-establishing itself
in Broadland early this century, following its extinction in most areas
by the middle of last century, the bittern still has the large reedbeds of
Norfolk and Suffolk as its British headquarters. There, early in the year,
the male of this strange elusive species is heard proclaiming his presence
by a booming note which will carry three or four miles. Many of the
bittern's haunts are nature reserves and at one of them, Minsmere, this
predatory bird is known to have destroyed nestlings of the marsh harrier,
a very scarce species of reedbeds whose extinction in Britain may be
imminent.

Grebes

Itself reduced, largely by the plume-trade, to only 42 pairs in England
in 1860, the great crested grebe later increased under protection. In

Great crested grebe, a species which has increased under protection.

East Anglia it now breeds on Broads, larger Breckland meres, flooded gravel pits and lakes, moving to the coast and estuaries in autumn and remaining there until about February. The diver (to use its descriptive local name) feeds mainly on small fish, but it needs a sufficient depth of water in which to gather speed enough to catch them. Great crested grebes are particularly attractive when the curiously striped young are being carried on the parents' backs.

More skulking than other grebes, the little grebe (or dabchick) may remain hidden in reedbeds during the breeding season, but 'rafts' of up to 40 or 50 of these excellent little divers may be seen on estuaries and pits near the coast in autumn and winter.

Birds of prey   A little way back I mentioned the predicament of the marsh harrier, a very scarce and specially protected species, which is being harmed by the bittern, another specially protected bird still regarded as rare. The history of East Anglian birds of prey is full of such conflict, and as a

Sparrowhawk, a specially protected species whose decrease has been attributed to persecution and the use of toxic chemicals.

result one reads all too often beside a species' name 'formerly bred'.

This is so with the hen harrier whose breeding areas included the Fens and Broadland. What may have been one of the very last of these birds nesting in East Anglia was shot because the gamekeeper considered the pair to be 'a nuisance on his beat'. Let us not be smug simply because the hen harrier is now specially protected, for a male was shot while visiting Norfolk in 1969. Two years later low-flying aircraft were active for several days over the marshes at Horsey where hen harriers last bred in 1861. They may have caused the harriers to leave after the male had been observed carrying nesting material for a week.

Persecution by gamekeepers and egg collectors, reclamation of fens and heaths, heath fires and disturbance all contributed to the sharp decrease of East Anglia's breeding population of Montagu's harrier. This slender-winged bird of graceful flight still visits the region, but only the odd pair nests now.

A kestrel returns with food to her nest in an old church tower.

Sparrowhawk

Kestrel

Very few pairs of sparrowhawks have bred successfully in Norfolk and Suffolk in recent years. The decrease has been attributed to the use of toxic chemicals. Certainly scientists at Monks Wood Experimental Station reported that this species was still generally laying thin-shelled eggs in 1971. But that year, for the first time since 1964, some eggs were found without any detectable dieldrin, though the DDE residues continued to remain relatively high. Persecution of this specially protected species, whose prey include blue tits, blackbirds, green woodpeckers and woodpigeons, as well as partridges and young pheasants, has not stopped. In 1971 – to quote but one instance – a brood of newly hatched young was found shot in Norfolk.

Lacking the sparrowhawk's ability to manoeuvre noiselessly at high speed in woodland in pursuit of prey, the kestrel hovers over open land, ready to drop swiftly on field voles moving in the grass or small birds feeding on the ground. The windhover (as it is called here) has not recovered completely from the marked decline of 1959–63, when it virtually disappeared from certain farming areas, due, it has been suggested, to toxic chemicals. But the visitor to Broadland, Breckland or the coastal belt stands a particularly good chance of seeing this graceful bird whose population and breeding success, like those of the barn owl, fluctuate

in some areas according to the abundance of its main prey, the short-tailed field vole.

Six species of owls breed in Britain and only one, the snowy owl, does not do so in East Anglia. Some of them are very scarce and all are now protected by law, the barn owl receiving special protection.

The commonest and most nocturnal British owl, the tawny owl, also called brown or wood owl, is well represented here. Despite the fact that it sometimes takes pheasant poults at night, this bird is a friend of gamekeepers and farmers, destroying large numbers of rats, mice and rabbits. The continued use of pole traps against tawny owls and other birds (*all* birds that land on them are maimed or killed) is a national disgrace. This vicious and cruel device was made illegal as long ago as 1904. But during the first three months of 1973 the R.S.P.B. received reports of pole traps on five estates and one farm in East Anglia. Unfortunately it is often difficult to prove who set or used the trap and, under the law, the owner of an estate or the head of a shooting syndicate cannot be prosecuted.

Even the harmless barn owl has been ruthlessly persecuted and, owing to this and other causes, its numbers have fallen considerably. In 1971 barn owls were reported from 107 localities in Norfolk and

Tawny owls, destroyers of rats, mice and rabbits, are still killed by illegal pole traps in East Anglia.

Owls

Suffolk, including 39 breeding sites. Nests were found in church towers, ruins, derelict cottages and drainage mills, cattle sheds, barns, and in hollow trees. A lack of breeding sites was suggested as one reason for the long-term decline of Billy-whit – to use one of the barn owl's local names (others are Gill-hooter and Madge!). This situation is being remedied in Norfolk where, for instance, an open-topped hollow elm, suitable only for roosting, was made into a successful breeding site by covering the top with canvas and making a new side entrance.

In east Norfolk the examination of over 5,000 pellets of fur, feathers and bones of prey ejected by barn owls showed that field voles and common shrews formed almost all the prey when the birds hunted grassland. But in areas where hedgerows, woodland and arable land were present other species, such as bank voles and wood mice, formed a larger portion of the prey and field voles correspondingly less. So changing farming methods, involving, for example, destruction of hedgerows, affect the food supply of barn owls (not to mention other species).

Removal of old hollow hedgerow trees in which it once bred is probably one reason for the little owl's decrease. Certainly the sight of our smallest British owl perched on a post in broad daylight is not so familiar as it was. One of the earliest attempts to establish the little owl as a British breeding bird was made in Norfolk when Lord Kimberley released six in 1876–77. By 1946 the food of this species, now well established, was the subject of much controversy, enormous damage being alleged by gamekeepers. A great deal of the outcry against the little owl was based upon insufficient evidence and hearsay, but there were well informed people who thought that it was increasing too rapidly. Now (1974) the little owl is granted 'ordinary' legal protection and the Avian Predators Working Party feels that there should normally be no need for control.

The short-eared owl is frequently seen during the day, sometimes in brilliant sunshine, flying close to the ground, searching for voles, small birds and beetles. Its local name, marsh owl, reminds us that it nests on the ground, among grass or rushes, on marshes in Broadland, Breckland and the coastal belt. The young short-eared owl's ability to move the whole facial disc till the eyes are vertical (a habit of old birds, too, occasionally) is particularly interesting.

Unlike the last species, the long-eared owl prefers coniferous woods and thorn thickets where it nests in trees, in old squirrels' dreys or old nests of crows, pigeons, jays or sparrowhawks, and rarely on the ground. It is not often seen in the daytime, but towards evening it emerges from cover in search of food. Known locally as horned owl, from its prominent ear-tufts, it breeds at Hickling, in Breckland and near parts of the coast.

Birds of prey and certain other birds (not to mention mammals – See chapter 4) have been persecuted and, as we have seen, some are still harassed. In East Anglia much of this activity was (and still is) in the supposed interests of game-birds and their pursuers. In some quarters, predators are still regarded as 'vermin', as happened last century, and it is sometimes more 'convenient' to kill them than to devise means of protecting gamebirds. In *Predatory Birds in Britain*, the Avian Predators Working Party deals with the protection of wild gamebirds, stating that it should always be the long-term aim to improve cover for safe nesting and escape and other habitat requirements. Concerned with the protection of reared gamebirds, too, it discusses 'scaring' devices as deterrents to tawny owls, sparrowhawks and other predators. *Game-birds*

Protection

East Anglia has a long tradition of game preservation. In 1803, for example, clumps of woodland were planted on heathland at Weeting, because there was too little cover for pheasants, which flourished in the new conditions (as did rabbits!). First introduced into England before 1059, the pheasant was originally a bird of well-wooded hill- and river-country with reedbeds. Colourful and conspicuous, it is a common resident in Broadland, roosting and nesting in reedbeds and amongst tussock sedges, eating seeds, berries and leaves of marsh plants. Pheasants are plentiful on farmland, too. Here they find wireworms, worms and insects, also eating newly sown corn and peas, sometimes taking as much as woodpigeons or rooks. When disturbed pheasants run for cover or rise noisily into the air. They will also swim, even when it is not necessary! *Pheasants*

In Breckland, where several of them were released by large landowners at intervals over the past 75 or 85 years, golden pheasants have become established over a wide area. The first golden pheasant at large in Britain was reported in Norfolk in 1845. It was at first taken for a hybrid between a common pheasant and our next species, the red-legged partridge.

Frenchmen, as red-legged partridges are also known, began their continuous colonisation of England about 1790, when thousands of imported eggs were hatched at Sudbourne and Rendlesham, near the Suffolk coast. And by 1828 the red-leg outnumbered the grey (English) partridge on east Suffolk coastal heaths. Strange to relate there were times when redlegs' nests were destroyed in Norfolk and the old birds shot 'anyhow or at any season'. Apparently the redleg's habit of running in preference to flight angered certain 'sportsmen' who called it 'unsportsmanlike'! *Partridges*

For many years red-legs and grey partridges have occurred on the same East Anglian farmland, having the same diet, weed seeds of *Polygonum* species, particularly black bindweed *P. convolvulus*, being important items. The grey was said to be the commoner, but this species has declined in East Anglia where red-legs have shown a marked increase. It is suggested that some kind of interaction may be taking place in the case of the two species. Also red-leg chicks, hatching later than those of grey partridges, are believed to feed more effectively on cereal aphids, insects that have increased in number and importance as sawfly larvae and leaf-eating beetles, formerly foods of great value to partridges, have declined.

Quail

Decrease and decline are words often used in reference to the quail, Britain's smallest true game-bird. A summer visitor from the Mediterranean area and Africa, it is more easily heard than seen in cornfields and grassland. The call, liquid and musical, loud and clear, is often written as 'Wet-mi'lips'.

Corncrake

The corncrake, Raffle Jack of Norfolk and Suffolk, has suffered through farm mechanisation and is common only in parts of Britain where hay is still produced by older methods and early cuts of grass are not taken for silage. In East Anglia corncrakes are rarely reported nowadays except when found dead or injured, sometimes by flying into telegraph lines.

Water rail

Also 'telegraphed' from time to time, the water rail is an elusive species of swamps and reedbeds. Revealing its presence by shrill squeals, it prefers thick cover and is often reluctant to take wing. During hard weather, water rails, among the first birds to perish then, have been seen away from their normal haunts, feeding on dead birds and coypus.

Moorhen

More often called waterhen here, the moorhen is common and familiar on East Anglian waters. But familiarity breeds contempt and many people ignore this handsome bird whose 'hairy' variety, with plumage resembling hair rather than feathers, is seen in the region. Though protected during the close season (1st February to 31st August, both dates inclusive), the moorhen may occasionally be controlled at other times. Feeding mainly on plant material, it also takes worms, snails, larvae and other animal matter. Plant food may include winter wheat and pasture, both heavily grazed at times, while young birds and eggs may appear among animal food taken.

Coot

A bird of open waters, baldie-coot, to use the coot's local name, is not seen on land as much as the moorhen. Quarrelsome and aggressive, coots often bully moorhens in Broadland. Even great crested grebes, birds coots like to nest near, are driven away at times.

Woodpigeon

Unfriendliness has long been the official attitude towards woodpigeons, landowners and farmers being expected to destroy them and their nests whenever possible. But campaigns against these birds have sometimes helped another pest, as when, a few winters ago, pigeon carcases dumped in Norfolk hedgerows formed survival rations for large numbers of rats. In 1961 the pigeon menace forced a Walsingham, Norfolk, farmer to sell 400 ewes and lambs, as large flocks of pigeons had eaten the greenstuff on which the sheep fed. Three or four years earlier the same man sold 120 sucking cows and calves for the same reason. Since the mid-1960s the woodpigeon's numbers have fallen drastically as repeated cereal cropping has replaced the Norfolk 4-course rotation system whose clover is the critical winter food to which population size is adjusted. A good word (if it can truthfully be called good) about woodpigeons comes from scientists of Monks Wood Experimental Station, who regard them as 'an agency whereby large quantities of toxic seed-dressings are removed from the environment'.

Stock dove

Often feeding with woodpigeon flocks in winter, stock doves search old stubbles and open bare ground for weed and grass seeds. Formerly nesting in disused rabbit-holes and tunnels in rabbit-cropped gorse in Breckland, they later took to ruined buildings in the Stanford Practical Training Area. Elsewhere in East Anglia stock doves nest in broad-leaved woods, while in Suffolk they have bred in disused pipes at a sewage farm.

Turtle dove

Unlike the last two birds, both residents, the turtle dove is a summer visitor. Not surprisingly, its distribution is similar to that of its main food, fumitory (*Fumaria*), a common weed of arable land and waste places. Nesting in overgrown hedges, thickets, tall gorse bushes and young conifers, turtle doves have decreased in parts of East Anglia with hedge destruction. But Breckland, with its conifer plantations and hedges of Scots pine and spruce, is one stronghold. Broadland is another, its fen carrs having bushes and trees that suit coo-coo-roos (a local name).

Collared dove

Turtle doves and their 'restful summer music' have long been known in East Anglia. But a new bird was added to the national list when collared doves first arrived and bred in Norfolk in 1955. They have since increased to such a remarkable extent that breeding occurs locally in most counties of Britain. The first breeding site was a small garden in Cromer where a pair reared two young. Four birds wintered there, taking grain put out for them during hard spells and visiting a nearby poultry run. In many other places the presence of poultry runs for feeding has helped these doves considerably. They like to be near houses and, being naturally wary, use television aerials, poles and electric cables as 'look-out' posts.

Crows

Turning to the crow family, I must first mention the magpie. This elegant bird, the subject of so much traditional folk-lore, has declined in East Anglia since about 1959. The most widely held reasons for this are the destruction of hedges, sites of many of its domed nests, the use of toxic chemicals, and possibly the extensive ploughing of old grassland where magpies eagerly hunt grasshoppers and find much other food.

Magpie

Their liking for eggs and young birds has got magpies a bad name, particularly in game rearing areas. And, like all the other birds mentioned in this section on crows, they may be killed or taken by authorised persons.

Jay

Unlike the magpie, the jay has not declined. But like the magpie it will take eggs and young birds and as a result this colourful bird is often seen on East Anglian gamekeepers' gibbets. A woodland bird, the jay's primary diet is acorns. Many acorns are buried in hiding places in the ground where some develop into seedlings. Well able to recognise oak seedlings, the jay digs down and, without damaging the young tree, removes the cotyledons, the food leaves of the acorn. When feeding their young, jays and magpies take large numbers of defoliating caterpillars and other insects. But this fact may be overlooked when narrow sectional interests are discussed and such emotive words as pest and vermin are bandied about.

Rook

With its long-disputed economic status, the rook is another much maligned species, though there are many areas where, and times when, it is not really harmful. A bird of grassland and arable farmland, the rook is a prober and, when necessary, a digger. It does take grain and eggs (including those of other rooks), but large numbers of earthworms, beetles, flies, caterpillars and leatherjackets are also eaten. Fortunately there are still many places in East Anglia where one may observe the noisy activity of rooks or 'crows', as they are so often called.

Jackdaw

Often in company with rooks and roosting with them in winter, jackdaws forage on grassland, seeking insects, worms, snails and other foods. Their liking for young birds and eggs may cause damage to shooting interests, but their high-pitched call, 'tchack', enlivens places where they nest in old hollow trees, church towers, ruined and derelict buildings.

Carrion Crow

In parts of East Anglia game-preservation is believed to have checked the increase of carrion crows whose feeding habits can cause considerable damage to shooting interests. But it is possible to see them in winter flocks, seventy having roosted at Roydon Common where they mobbed the hen harriers, a winter feature at this Norfolk reserve. Elsewhere in East Anglia carrion crows have taken eggs and young of mallard, terns, oystercatchers, black-headed gulls and other birds.

Starlings

One of the world's most successful birds, the starling probes grass roots and soil in search of leatherjackets, beetles, wireworms and other small creatures. But, always ready to take whatever is available, it also eats grain, cherries, and food put out for cattle and poultry (sometimes causing serious damage) and, in Broadland, coypu dropping. Starlings may be killed or taken by authorised persons, but they are common and thriving birds here.

Green woodpecker
feeding young.

Vast numbers roost in Broadland reedbeds in autumn, moving to winter roosts in plantations and thickets in December. At dusk it is fascinating to watch as they return to roost from foraging grounds up to thirty miles away. Numerous small flocks coalesce into bigger ones. These contract and expand, snake and weave, in fantastic aerial dances. Then the birds drop down in their thousands to bathe and drink before settling in the trees. The sheer weight of starlings breaks tops off trees, while that of accumulated droppings damages lower branches. On the ground deep guano affects vegetation and provides cover for burrowing rats, which emerge to drag away dead and dying birds.

Starlings plague green and great spotted woodpeckers, sometimes evicting them from their newly-excavated holes in tree trunks. These two woodpeckers and also the lesser spotted woodpecker, a scarcer species, inhabit wooded places, especially those where old trees occur. All three are found in Broadland carrs. The food of woodpeckers consists

Woodpeckers

Kingfisher at Minsmere, one of many East Anglian localities where this fast-flying bird is seen.

mainly of insects and it is while searching for boring insects in wood that is usually already decaying that they attack trees. Woodpeckers occasionally kill young tits and other nestlings. But, as if to redress the balance, their holes are used as nesting sites by tits, nuthatches and other hole-nesting birds.

Orioles

Sometimes confused with the green woodpecker because of its undulating flight, the golden oriole is a tree-bird whose buttercup yellow and glossy black male gives a brilliant flash in the sun. It has yet to establish itself as a regular breeding bird in Britain, but breeding was attempted in north-west Suffolk in 1967 when a nest in an alder tree contained one egg, which was later found broken. At a locality on the Breck borders in Norfolk, where at least one golden oriole was present each summer from 1967 to 1971, young were found in 1972. A pair had returned there in May and a second male was present in June. It is a pity that this beautiful bird, whose whistle has been regarded as the most human of all bird whistles, is more often heard than seen.

Kingfishers

Like the cock oriole, the kingfisher gives a magnificent flash in the sun. A fast-flying bird, it is seen along rivers, streams and other waters (including garden pools) in many parts of East Anglia. Although kingfishers may move to the Broads or dykes and tidal creeks on the coast in autumn, hard weather takes a heavy toll of them. Sadly this is inevitable, for they feed mainly on small fishes captured during darting dives, an activity demanding open water. The kingfisher generally nests in a stream-bank, laying its glossy white eggs in a circular chamber at the end of a short tunnel. But in Suffolk a few years ago a pair of kingfishers reared four young in the side of a deep hole twenty yards inside a wood and 440 yards from a river. The hole was only two feet in diameter and surrounded by metal railings.

Like the kingfisher, the sand martin generally makes a horizontal burrow with a nesting chamber at the end. Nesting in colonies, sand martins tunnel into the faces of sand-pits and sea cliffs (as at Dunwich, Suffolk). But they have nested in huge sawdust piles at Breckland saw-mills and in sand bunkers at Flempton, Suffolk, golf-course. Nesting under eaves of houses, house martins are familiar summer residents in many East Anglian towns and villages, where as many as 70–80 nests have been counted on a single building. Although mud is generally used for nest building, house martins near Norwich used a mixture of cement and sand from a building site, despite the presence of a muddy pond.

Swallows often nest on beams in barns, garages and other roofed buildings. In Norfolk they have also nested in below-ground military emplacements, while elsewhere in the county they reared young in a nest on top of a curtain pelmet. Unlike martins and swallows, swifts indulge in wild screaming forays above and around buildings on summer

*Martins, swifts
and swallows*

evenings. They usually nest in church towers and other buildings, but a few still do so in cliffs at Hunstanton, Norfolk. Martins, swifts and swallows feed on flying insects and normally move south to warmer countries before their food supply is drastically reduced with the arrival of winter. Even so, late birds are observed in Norfolk and Suffolk. Last dates for 1972 were:

Sand martin	October 24	Snettisham, Norfolk.
House martin	December 5	Sizewell, Suffolk.
Swallow	*December 16	Upwell, Norfolk.
Swift	October 29	Caister-on-Sea, Norfolk.

*On this date (while wintering in pig sheds) the bird was killed by a cat.

Some other summer visitors

Cuckoo

Many other summer visitors which come to Britain to breed also feed entirely or mainly on insects. They, too, must leave this country before their food becomes extremely difficult, if not impossible, to find. One, the cuckoo, 'the bird of spring', arrives in East Anglia early in April and 'late' birds may be seen during the first 7–10 days of October. Nowadays it is not common in farming areas. This may partly be due to the low density there of dunnocks and meadow pipits, important foster parents to the 'parasitic' bird whose eggs have been recorded in nests of over fifty species. The cuckoo's call is much more likely to be heard now in uncultivated parts of Broadland, Breckland and the coastal belt.

Nightingale

It is no longer considered important to hear the song of the nightingale before that of the cuckoo. But despite a decline in places, due partly to the destruction of thick hedgerows and copses, nightingales are still heard in East Anglia. I was kept awake at night by these mastersingers at Old Buckenham, on the edge of the Norfolk Breckland, where nightingales were also heard in broad daylight in the grounds of a boys' preparatory school. More recently I have enjoyed the song of nightingales at Foulden Common, also in the Norfolk Breckland.

Blackcap

With its outstanding purity of voice and range of high, flute-like notes, the blackcap is sometimes regarded as a more notable songster than the nightingale. A bird of woodland, including Broadland carrs and Breckland pine plantations, it was formerly regarded as being purely a summer visitor and passage migrant. But individuals have been seen in the 'wrong' months (November – March, inclusive) in several parts of East Anglia. With insects very scarce, winter blackcaps turn to fruits and berries, and even take fat, scraps and chipped peanuts at garden bird-tables. Care should be taken not to record small black-capped tits, marsh and willow tits, as blackcaps. Also one must remember that 'blackcap' is an East Anglian local name of the reed bunting.

Chiffchaff

Most chiffchaffs have left East Anglian woodlands by early October, but wintering individuals are noticed here in December and January. They do not appear to visit bird-tables, but have been seen feeding on

These young reed
warblers fledged
successfully despite
the fact that a gale
beat down the reeds
supporting their nest.

Warblers

elder berries. Best identified by its song, because in general appearance
it so closely resembles the chiffchaff, the willow warbler eats many
defoliating caterpillars, but it will take berries in autumn. The willow
warbler is not given to wintering in East Anglia. Usually singing while
hidden in dense bushes, the garden warbler nests in open woodland
where undergrowth is present. But the wood warbler, a decreasing
species in East Anglia, prefers woods with little undergrowth.

Reed warblers are abundant summer visitors to reedbeds by broads,
lakes, ponds and rivers. Expert and graceful gymnasts, these 'nightingales of the Broads' grasp swaying reeds, standing upside down to
feed their nestlings. Suspended between four or five reeds deep in a
dense reedbed, the nest is somewhat frail in appearance but wind resist-
ing, swaying as the reeds sway. In Broadland the reed warbler often uses
fluff from sallow catkins in the nest's outer part, while at Aldeburgh,
Suffolk, two nests almost entirely of sheep's wool were once seen.

Unlike reed warblers, sedge warblers are not restricted to reedbeds, though many do nest there. They also breed in sedge fens, bushy marshes, damp ditches and even in cornfields and other dry places. As singers, chatterers and mimics, they enliven reedbed and marsh alike.

Savi's warbler, an inhabitant of extensive reedswamps, is not unlike a reed warbler, though there are important differences. Its song, a reel or trill, differs from the grasshopper warbler's in that low ticking notes precede it. Savi's warbler ceased to be a regular summer visitor to East Anglia, where it had nested in small numbers, about the middle of last century. Then in 1970 breeding was proved ar Walberswick and the following year at Minsmere, too. Now there is a chance of additional colonies being established on other protected marshes in East Anglia.

In Broadland the grasshopper warbler's distinctive song earned it the name of reeler. Miss E. L. Turner, the distinguished ornithologist who lived in a Broadland houseboat among the birds she watched and photographed, said this referred to the sound made by the reel formerly used by the hand spinners of wool and *not* to the 'spinning' of a fisherman's reel. Besides the swampy carrs of Broadland, the shy and inconspicuous grasshopper warbler visits marshy places in river valleys and in the coastal belt, and grassy bushy heaths and commons.

It was once said that the grasshopper warbler's only claim to be a warbler was that it belonged to the family of that name. Both whitethroat and lesser whitethroat are warblers which do, in fact, warble, though the whitethroat has been accused of 'gabbling'. A bird of hedgerows, overgrown ditches and low scrub, the whitethroat is also fond of nettle beds, as its East Anglian names, nettle warbler and nettle creeper, testify. The lesser whitethroat prefers tall, coarse hedges and thickets. The insects taken by whitethroats include butterflies whose wings are quickly removed. In 1949, when Dr. Edward Ellis, the Norfolk naturalist and television personality, was trying to establish these magnificent insects at Wheatfen Broad, Norfolk, whitethroats caught and ate the bodies of female large copper butterflies.

Spotted flycatcher

Butterflies and moths are among the insects taken by the spotted flycatcher, one of the very last of our summer visitors to arrive. A bird of parks, gardens and woods, it is readily identified by its habit of making repeated short flights from its favourite perch to snap up insects. Two of its East Anglian local names, wall-bird and beam-bird, tell us something of its nesting habits, while another, bee-bird, refers to the fact that it takes bees occasionally. One of the greatest enemies of bumblebees is the red-backed shrike. Impaling surplus food on thorns, it is also called the butcher-bird. A summer visitor, usually arriving a little later than the spotted flycatcher, it is no longer common. Nowadays it is mainly a bird of Breckland and the coastal belt.

Red-backed Shrike

Wheatear

Wheatears were once common and characteristic birds of Breckland

This nightjar was photographed while singing at night.

and plentiful summer visitors to heaths, coastal warrens and dunes. They are now best known in East Anglia as passage migrants. Afforestation in Breckland covered open stony places where wheatears bred with trees, making them unsuitable. Destruction of rabbits by foresters and myxomatosis allowed pines, birches and other vegetation to spread, rendering other places unsuitable. And the filling in of rabbit holes and lack of new ones caused a serious loss of nesting sites for breeding 'burrow-birds'. The disappearance of sheep from East Anglian heaths allowed vegetation to develop and also played a part in the decline of breeding 'shepherd birds' (to use yet another of the wheatear's local names). Happily, experiments with grazing sheep and rabbits are in progress at Thetford and Weeting heaths, both breeding sites for wheatears. At these Breckland National Nature Reserves, empty ammunition boxes have been sunk into the ground to provide nesting sites for wheatears.

Unlike the wheatear, the whinchat, a decreased species here, favours rough neglected pastures and other areas of coarse vegetation. Its local names – furze-chat, furze-chuck and furze hacker (names also applied to the stonechat) – give a clue to the kind of place where it may be seen in the coastal belt and Breckland.

Whinchat

Nightjar

These two areas, especially Breckland, remain strongholds of the declining nightjar. Here heaths, commons, open woods and dry bracken areas are favoured. But myxomatosis, with its destruction of rabbits and the subsequent growth of coarse vegetation, caused many sites to be abandoned by this ground-nester. The nightjar is active mostly from dusk to dawn, the period during which the 'big razor-grinder's' continuous churring song is heard.

Redstart

Deciduous woods in Breckland are where one is most likely to find redstarts, though they still breed in other parts of East Anglia. Formerly abundant summer residents, even nesting in the heart of Norwich, they are far from common now. The redstart is known locally as fire-tail because of its quivering fiery tail, but the name redstart itself simply means red-tail from the Old English steort (= tail).

Black Redstart

The closely related black redstart first nested in East Anglia, probably in Ipswich, in 1938, but has since done so in a number of towns on the coast and also inland. During the 1940s and 1950s this scarce species nested in bombed buildings and air-raid shelters. It now makes use of the power station at Sizewell, on the Suffolk coast, and buildings in Ipswich docks area, Yarmouth, Norwich, and a few other places.

Tree pipit
Wagtails

The tree pipit, a wasteland species of heaths and commons, and the yellow wagtail, whose nests are built in situations as varied as under tufts of dead grass on Broadland grazing levels, amongst heather in Breckland, and in *Suaeda* bushes on Scolt Head Island, are summer visitors whose numbers are down. Yellow wagtails are known to remain faithful to their old breeding areas unless conditions become completely impossible. In Suffolk, for example, they nested on heathland and continued to do so among potato crops ten years after it was reclaimed for cultivation. Their East Anglian name, cow-bird, reminds us that yellow wagtails take many flies attracted by the droppings of grazing cattle.

Although, unlike yellow wagtails, many remain here in winter, pied wagtails also live largely on flies and other insects. Their diet often takes them to the waterside and places where animals are kept. In winter pied wagtails may visit manure heaps and greenhouses, where insects may be active, and gardens (even window-sills) whose owners provide crumbs. Flocks of these graceful birds may roost in greenhouses, but in East Anglia it is more usual to find them forming communal winter roosts in reedbeds. Pied wagtails often select safe nesting sites on buildings. But in Norfolk one pair took over a large flowerpot in a cool greenhouse, though, even here, the nest was discovered by a cuckoo, which duly left its egg. More recently, at Yaxham, Norfolk, pied wagtails reared young in a nest built on the engine of a cement mixer, despite the fact that the machine was in regular use.

Although it is not a common breeding species here, the grey wagtail (which should not be confused with the shorter-tailed yellow wagtail) is present in East Anglia throughout the year, and has even been seen in the centre of Norwich.

No strangers to the centres of East Anglian towns, including Norwich, where a pair reared young in a crack in the castle battlements recently, blue tits are both abundant and widespread. Seen in almost every garden of any size, they feed, particularly in winter, on peanuts, coconut, fat and many other foods put out by bird-lovers. True they do sometimes spoil their reputation as lively and entertaining acrobats by opening milk-bottles and pilfering cream and by tearing wallpaper. In summer they make up for this in the woods, where they nest in holes and nest-boxes, by eating thousands of insect larvae. At that time of year these larvae represent only a small proportion of the total. But at Thetford it has been shown that tits and other birds eat a substantial proportion of the insect population in winter.

Tits

Like its smaller relative, the great tit, another common garden-visitor, is largely an insect eater. Even honey-bees are taken occasionally, a fact embodied in its local name, bee-bird (also applied to the blue tit). Nesting in suitable holes, great tits are attracted to large conifer plantations such as Thetford Forest, where holes may be scarce, by the use of nest boxes. The coal tit, the commonest tit of coniferous woods, also makes great use of nesting boxes at Thetford Forest and elsewhere. But, the smallest of its group, it is quite content with a mouse-hole in a bank or even a tiny chink in a wall. An insect-eater, it will however visit bird tables in winter.

Marsh and willow tits are frequently confused with one another, though their songs and their typical call-notes are quite different. Strictly speaking, neither are garden birds, but in winter they are occasionally reported at bird-tables (even the window-sill variety) where the marsh tit can be most confiding and the willow tit a little bully! Despite their name, marsh tits are primarily birds of deciduous woods. Willow tits have strongholds in Broadland and marshland carrs and also in Breckland. Like coal tits, marsh and willow tits will hide food away, sometimes only to have it stolen by great tits.

Long-tailed tits do not often venture into gardens except in the country, though severe weather, when they suffer badly, may bring them there. Hedgerow destruction is believed to account for their decrease in some parts of East Anglia. Tidying operations also upset this small species of deciduous woods with undergrowth, thickets, bushy commons and uncultivated areas of the coastal belt. The roving flocks of long-tailed tits seen in woods and hedgerows in winter begin to break up in February when pairs form. Often beginning in March, nest building is shared by both partners. The nest, an oval ball with an entrance near the top on one side, is decorated with lichens and lined

A bearded tit visits its nest low in the reeds.

with 2,000 or more feathers. One of the long-tailed tit's East Anglian names, featherpoke, refers to this lining, while two others, pudding-poke and oven-bird, refer to the shape of the nest (poke = a bag).

The bearded tit's local names, reed-pheasant and bearded reedling, are equally apt. This attractive and agile bird of extensive Broadland and coastal reedbeds was almost lost to Britain on a number of occasions, egg and bird collectors, severe winters, drainage of marshlands and sea floods, having all caused setbacks from time to time. A particularly heavy toll was taken by the blizzards of early 1947 when, like many other areas, Hickling and its reedbeds, home of a bearded tit colony, was buried in several feet of snow. The only bearded tits to survive this hard winter in East Anglia, then the species' sole territory in Britain, were a single male in Norfolk and one or two pairs in Suffolk. By 1962, by which time small colonies had also become established in Essex and Kent, 285 pairs of bearded tits were known to be breeding in East Anglia. They were not so disastrously affected by the severe winter of early 1963,

Reed bunting bringing food to nestlings. Formerly regarded as a wetland species, this bird also breeds in dry places now.

largely because there was not such a great depth of snow as in 1947. All the same, the population was more than halved. Many survived by eating reed seeds, and, as is their custom in winter, they followed the reed-cutters for food. By 1965 the East Anglian breeding population had again increased, this time to an estimated 257 pairs. In 1972 about 80 pairs bred on the freshwater marsh at Minsmere, while in Norfolk there were breeding colonies at Hickling Broad and several other Broadland sites, Cley and Titchwell. In a season bearded tits may rear as many as three, or even four, broods, feeding them on insects at their nests low in the reeds. The young, having to fend for themselves early in life, roam about the reedbeds in little parties. After the breeding season, old and young together wander in Broadland and sometimes further afield.

Young reed buntings, too, soon become independent, living for a time in little groups in reedbeds, scrub and other cover. Once regarded as strictly wetland birds of Broadland reed and sedge beds, marshes and river valleys, reed buntings are now also found breeding in much drier

Buntings

habitats, including heather and young conifer plantations in Breckland. They have also nested near the ground in marram-grass tussocks and in *Suaeda* bushes on Scolt Head Island. Handsome in his breeding plumage, the male is a disappointing singer, its efforts resulting in little more than a monotonous stuttering.

Some of the dry places into which reed buntings have been moving are typical habitats of the yellowhammer (or yellow bunting), farmland with hedgerows, scrubby rough land, bushy roadside banks, commons and edges of open woods. With its brilliant yellow head and under-parts, the male yellowhammer is most attractive, but the female is much browner and dull. Seeds, blackberries and insects all form part of this common bird's diet.

Like the yellowhammer, the corn bunting is said to have been known in East Anglia as gule and guler. There has been some argument as to the use and origin of these names, but another local name, leg dangler, obviously refers to the male corn bunting's habit of often flying with its legs dangling. Birds of open ground, large fields and wasteland, corn buntings have a curious patchy distribution, colonies being found in East Anglia in the coastal belt, the Fens and in and around Breckland. Feeding mainly on vegetable matter and insects, they were seen giving ivy berries to their nestlings in Broadland.

Lapland and snow buntings are winter visitors to the East Anglian coast, north Norfolk and Breydon being well favoured. They spend much of their time searching stubbles, saltings, grazing marshes, sand-dunes and tidelines for seeds. Nowadays these buntings are not molested, but at one time large numbers were netted and shot, particularly at Yarmouth.

Blackbirds and thrushes

Like corn buntings, mentioned earlier, blackbirds and thrushes have been known to feed ivy berries to their young. Like other true thrushes, they are often ignored by Bird Reports and even general naturalists despite the fact that they are interesting creatures whose activities can be important, if only locally, at times. For example, blackbirds and song thrushes can cause considerable damage to ripening fruit, pecking holes through which wasps and fungus spores gain entry.

The blackbird, probably the commonest song-bird in Britain, was originally a woodland bird. But it is now found breeding on farmland with hedges, in gardens and city centres, and even on Blakeney Point and Scolt Head Island. Hedges, bushes and ivy-covered trees and buildings are often selected as nesting sites, but many unusual ones are on record. In East Anglia blackbirds have nested in a busy and noisy forge, in a lorry (delaying delivery), and at the top of a vibrating hydraulic vehicle lift post (young were successfully reared). But one of the most extraordinary stories concerned blackbirds at Acle, Norfolk, whose nest was beneath a railway truck laden with anthracite. Each time 'the black-birds' truck' was emptied the nest was moved to the loaded truck that replaced it. Eight moves and still three eggs hatched!

Certainly blackbirds *are* adaptable, apparently more so than song thrushes over changes brought about by man. Where food is concerned, blackbirds are prepared to make use of whatever suitable types are readily available. They will, for example, feed their first broods largely on earthworms in March and April, changing to caterpillars for later broods in May and June. Again, when animal food is scarce, they eat many kinds of berries and also crab and waste apples.

In the 1960s a male blackbird was seen catching minnows and break-ing them to pieces before swallowing them or carrying them away. A male song thrush fished from the same narrow concrete ledge whose surface was just covered by lapping water. It took minnows one year, but the following year it seized a little dace, banging it on the brickwork before swallowing it whole.

Like the blackbird, the song thrush was originally a woodland bird. Since adapted even to treeless areas, it is now a bird of hedgerows, parks, gardens, orchards and farmland, and it has nested on Scolt Head Island. During 'starvation weather' song thrushes feed on berries and their ability to open snails on anvils (stones and other firm, flat surfaces) is useful then.

Unlike the song thrush, the mistle thrush is a very aggressive species, attacking jays, magpies, cats and even people who venture too close to its young. A bird of parks, orchards, large gardens and open woodland, the storm-cock, as the mistle thrush is known for this very reason, will continue to pour out its loud free song throughout the wildest of weather.

Two other members of the thrush family, fieldfare and redwing, are winter visitors from northern Europe. Seen on marshes and farmland and in woods, orchards and hedgerows, they feed on berries and apples when worms, slugs and other animal food are not available. By dropping seeds from these fruits, which pass through their bodies unharmed, they spread various berry-bearing shrubs. During the arctic weather of early 1963, when many redwings perished here, fieldfares and redwings visited town gardens in large numbers. In the centre of Norwich red-wings foraged beneath market-stalls and close by, on Guildhall Green, some were fed by taxi-drivers.

Another winter visitor from northern Europe is the brambling, one of the finches. Although numbers vary from year to year, good 'beech-mast years' tending to be good 'brambling years', it can be seen during most winters feeding under beeches, often with its close relative, the chaffinch. Beech belts in and around Breckland are favoured, as are Breckland conifer plantations where fallen pine seeds are taken. Farming

Finches

areas also attract flocks of bramblings, and hundreds feed in mustard-fields and on seed kale. Bramblings are seen in East Anglian towns, too, gardens in the middle of Bury St Edmunds and Norwich being among those visited. With their deeper and sharper bills, bramblings can open beech nuts more easily than chaffinches. This does not seem to create unhealthy competition between them as normally they only consort with one another when food is plentiful.

Largely ignored by the Bird Reports and, as *Birds* put it, 'Too common to be well known', chaffinches are still abundant breeding birds in East Anglia despite the destruction on arable farmland of many hedgerows, commonly selected nesting sites. Usually built in trees or bushes, the nest is camouflaged by bits of lichens on the outside. This material was even used by chaffinches nesting in the corner of a garden shed, an unusual site for this species. Known in East Anglia as 'spink', undoubtedly from its call-note, a brisk 'pink, pink', the chaffinch rears its young on animal matter, mainly caterpillars and other leaf-insects. Outside the breeding season, its main food is seeds, including spilled grain and also weed-seeds from the surface of freshly-turned soil. In autumn and winter large numbers of immigrant chaffinches arrive here. They feed in open country and are also seen at large roosts in conifers and thickets.

Unlike these fringilline finches (brambling and chaffinch), the cardueline finches discussed below – hawfinch, greenfinch, goldfinch, siskin, linnet, redpoll, crossbill and bullfinch – rear their young mainly (but not always entirely) on seeds. So these finches are able to breed even when insects are scarce.

Hawfinches feed their young every 7–8 minutes, regurgitating seeds into their mouths or carrying insects to them in their bills. The cobble-bird (a name given to the hawfinch because its powerful beak enables it to crack stones, or cobbles, of cherries and similar fruit) breeds in woodland, orchards and large gardens, but is shy and elusive. During recent winters hawfinches have been seen feeding in hornbeams and yews in Breckland.

In autumn and winter flocks of greenfinches visit fields, wasteland, marsh walls and river banks, picking seeds from plants and the ground. Some venture into gardens and eat peanuts, often clinging to containers suspended from branches and bird-tables. I have seen them doing this close to a busy main road. I have also watched greenfinches in Norwich and the village of Ringland, Norfolk, feeding on the round red berries of *Daphne mezereum*, a shrub whose fragrant pink flowers appear early in the year. In each case this happened close to the front door of a house. The greenfinch nests in bushes and is widespread and common.

Like the last species, the linnet and lesser redpoll have short and broad bills, though they have smaller ones and eat smaller seeds than the greenfinch. The linnet, which is intermediate in these respects, likes seeds from weeds of arable farmland, but also feeds in weedy gardens and on wasteland. In bushy places, gorse bushes are favourite nesting sites of linnets, which nest in *Suaeda* bushes and marram tussocks on Scolt Head Island. With a small bill, the lesser redpoll eats small seeds, including those of birch, certain weeds and grasses. Breeding in birch scrub, young conifer plantations and thickets, lesser redpolls often build their large untidy nests in tall bushes.

Goldfinches feed from dandelions, thistles and other plants of the family *Compositae*. And, with their long pointed bills, they are the only finches able to reach the seeds of teazles. Goldfinches often select large isolated trees for nesting, building on boughs high above the ground. Colourful and agile, graceful and dancing in flight, goldfinches are a joy to watch, especially in autumn and winter when charms of these birds search wasteland, gardens, weedy allotments and odd corners (even roadside verges) for seeds, and visit alders in the carrs of Broadland in company with redpolls and siskins. After the breeding season goldfinches often roost communally, and at Thorpe St Andrews, Norfolk, a roost in evergreen oaks and hollies held 500 by mid-January in 1973.

Siskins eat seeds of spruce, pine, elm, dandelion and other plants, and share the goldfinch's ability to feed from thistles by piercing and probing into the seed-heads. Visiting bird-tables to feed on fat, nuts and seeds, they are seen in gardens in many parts of East Anglia. With their main breeding grounds still in northern Britain, siskins are now breeding in several new forest areas further south. And it is encouraging to note that these include Breckland, where a few pairs have nested successfully in recent years, one 55 feet up in a Scots pine.

Breckland, with its conifer forests and shelterbelts, is also favoured by crossbills whose numbers are sometimes small and appear to depend upon periodical reinforcement by immigrants from the Continent. Nesting high in trees, often roadside pines, crossbills build early in the year, February and March being the main months for laying, though fledglings have been seen in Breckland as early as mid-January. Keeping largely to the tops of trees, crossbills may be detected by the frayed cones they drop after extracting the seeds (Unlike squirrels, they do not tear the scales off cones). In East Anglia they have also been seen feeding on aphids (greenfly), rowan berries, thistle seeds, poplar buds and, in a Great Fakenham garden, sunflower seeds. Crossbills have the reputation of being thirsty birds and they are known to drink from bird-baths. Breeding is not confined to Breckland, having been reported in the coastal belt, the neighbourhood of Norwich, and the Sandringham district from time to time.

Unlike the other finches mentioned, the bullfinch eats small snails in

Left Crossbills are
thirsty birds. This
one was photographed
at its drinking-place
in Rendlesham
Forest, Suffolk.

Right Hollesley
Heath, Suffolk, was
this individual's
habitat, but wrens
occur in many other
kinds of places.

Sparrows and dunnocks

quantity, but, with its short rounded beak, it tends to specialise on buds, berries and seeds. Buds form up to a third of its annual diet and, as many are taken from fruit trees at the rate of thirty or more per minute, considerable damage can be done in fruit-growing districts. Not surprisingly, the bullfinch, our only British finch of economic importance, is controlled in such areas. A common bird of hedges, thickets and scrubby woodland edges and undergrowth, the bullfinch has increased and spread into parks and gardens in recent years. Bullfinches breeding in woodland lose many eggs to jays, which sometimes force their way through thick brambles to reach nests.

Another bird which may cause trouble by destroying buds in orchards is the house sparrow, whose attacks on ornamental plants in spring are troublesome, too. After the breeding season, when house and tree sparrows often combine to form large flocks, sparrows feed in cornfields, picking grain from the ears of standing corn. But house and tree sparrows collect vast numbers of insects, especially when rearing their young, and both species take weed seeds. House sparrows commonly nest in holes or niches about houses, but at Shropham, Norfolk, a small colony nested in a blackthorn bush. Frequently overlooked, tree sparrows are less dependent on man and buildings. In East Anglia their nesting sites include the bottom of rooks' nests, hedgerows, pollarded trees, sand martins' holes in coastal cliffs and other convenient holes.

Often called hedge sparrow, the dunnock should not be confused with the sparrow species just mentioned. Neat, quiet but apparently always busy, this little bird has at least seven East Anglian names. Hedge Betty and Hedgemonger obviously refer to its liking for hedgerows and bushy places, while Shuffle-wing reminds us of the dunnock's curious way of flicking or 'shivering' its wings as it picks up seeds or tiny insects. Hatcher probably refers to the dunnock's positon as one of the cuckoo's chief fosterers, but what of udger or udgey?

Wren

Dunnocks are often said to be unsociable both among themselves and with other species. Wrens have much the same reputation, though there are times when they do associate with one another. During the hard winter of 1962–63 there were several reports of East Anglian wrens roosting together, one of over forty sheltering in a nest-box at Weston Longville, Norfolk. Wrens hunt insects and spiders in gardens, woodlands, hedgerows, rough marshes, Broadland reedswamps and many other types of habitat. Their nesting sites are just as varied. Young have been reared in an old hurricane lamp in a barn, a coil of rope hanging in a shed, a strawberry net (also hanging in a shed), old and new swallows' nests, the root masses of wind-felled trees, the centre of a broccoli plant, and hedges.

The robin and the wren, 'God Almighty's cock and hen', both choose unusual nesting sites, but the robin is perhaps bolder where people and their buildings are concerned. One pair even built on a pelmet in the lounge of a Hellesdon, Norfolk, house! Another robin used to enter a house, living largely on butter and magarine and feeding his mate and young on it. Normally the robin eats mainly insects, but also takes spiders, worms, seeds and soft fruits.

Robin

In 1960 the robin was chosen, as representative of all the birds of Britain, as a national symbol in work for bird protection. Certainly the robin is well known and well liked in East Anglia, where many a countryman still uses its old name, Bob. Food provided by bird-lovers helps many robins (and other birds) to survive hard winters. But many robins, some say 50–80 per cent, die then.

As we have already seen, several other insect-eating birds suffer during severe winters, some much more than the robin. One of them is the stonechat, whose call, like two pebbles being struck together, is heard on furzy heaths and commons and coastal dunes. Some habitats have been destroyed or rendered unsuitable by reclamation and tidying operations, and the reduction of the rabbit population allowed coarse vegetation to invade open areas where stonechats liked to feed. But hard winters in the 1940s virtually wiped out the stonechat in Breckland, once a stronghold of the species, and left only a few pairs in the coastal belt. Breeding stonechats are still very scarce and mainly confined to these two areas.

Other insect-eaters Stonechat

During hard weather treecreepers often suffer badly from lack of food. Highly specialised to a woodland life, treecreepers live on spiders, insects, their eggs and pupae. These are picked up as the bird climbs tree trunks and along the underside of boughs. Long, slender and down-curved, the treecreeper's beak is ideal for probing into tiny crevices and for searching behind loose bark. Treecreepers are not uncommon in wooded parts of East Anglia. They were observed roosting in hollows in the soft bark of Wellingtonia trees at Keswick Park, Norfolk, as long ago as 1926, and now do so in several other places in the region. Outside

Treecreeper

Arable farming attracts skylarks. This one visits its nestlings in a field of sugar-beet.

Nuthatches and goldcrests

the breeding season treecreepers often mix with roving parties of tits or goldcrests.

Unlike the treecreeper, which climbs but only occasionally creeps down them, the nuthatch habitually moves up *and down* tree trunks. A bird of deciduous woodlands, parks (even in towns) and large gardens, the nuthatch favours oaks and beeches in East Anglia, and their seeds, acorns and beechmast, form part of its diet. In autumn hazelnuts are taken, some for immediate consumption, others to be buried as reserves under dead leaves or in soft earth. Though less dependent on them than the treecreeper, the nuthatch also eats insects, including eggs of destructive moths.

Nuthatches are rare in conifers in Britain, but the goldcrest is very fond of these trees and plentiful in the Breckland conifer woods. A diet of spiders and insects means that the goldcrest, our smallest British bird, suffers badly during severe winters, though its numbers are made good within a few years. Goldcrests will allow quiet observers to stand within a few feet of them and will come to garden bird-tables. I have even heard of one taking suet from the hand, but this was not in East Anglia.

Larks and meadow pipits

The extensive planting of conifers in Breckland and elsewhere has undoubtedly helped the goldcrest. On the other hand, the woodlark, with its attachment to derelict sites of felled woodland, is sometimes regarded as an indicator of poor forestry. Be that as it may, such areas in Breckland and the coastal belt are haunts of this dumpy, short-tailed species, as are certain heaths. The woodlark's rapid decrease in some places has been attributed, partly at least, to habitats becoming overgrown following the loss of rabbits through myxomatosis. Many people who have known this bird regard its wild sweet song as the loveliest bird-sound in Britain. Delivered in flight or from a perch, this song inspired Phil Robinson, author of *The Poet's Birds*, to describe the woodlark as 'the one and only bird to whom the nightingale himself cannot give a note or presume to suggest a beauty.'

Like the woodlark, the skylark has inspired poets, its song, usually delivered on the wing, being both rich and vigorous. The skylark is abundant in open country in East Anglia, fields, heathland, grazing levels and coastal marram dunes (including those on Scolt Head Island) being among its habitats. Seeds, insects and worms form a large part of the lark's diet. It also grazes young seedlings, a habit occasionally leading to complaints in arable farming areas, where winter wheat at the chitting stage is eaten. Arable farming, with its cereal and root crops, attracts skylarks which favour ground thinly covered with grass or other suitable vegetation.

The meadow pipit prefers a ground cover of long grass, bracken or heather. In arable areas this species – the titlark or ground-lark of East Anglia – tends to nest only in rough waste corners. In Breckland it has disappeared from many places where conifers have replaced heather. But this small brown bird is still seen in Broadland where it nests on drier marshes and in other grassy places, Scolt Head Island and Minsmere being among its other breeding sites.

Ringing and migration

Ringing – the marking of birds by means of numbered metal leg-rings – yields information on such topics as migration routes, dispersal and life-span. In East Anglia it is carried out by registered ringers at several places (NB All ringers, trainees and helpers must obtain government licences through the British Trust for Ornithology before they can handle any birds).

Ringers from Holme bird observatory, Norfolk, which is open to visitors at certain times (See p.148), have ringed 18,974 birds of 126 species since it was established in 1962. Included in this grand total are 2,576 birds of 70 species ringed in 1972.

At Salthouse, Norfolk, the Walsey Hills ringing station is manned by the Norfolk Ornithologists' Association in spring and autumn. 1,260 birds of 59 species were ringed there in 1972, making a grand total of 4,460 birds of 76 species since 1970.

Ringers of the Dingle Bird Club operate at Walberswick, Suffolk. Those of the Wash Wader Ringing Group, who have ringed about 80,000 birds since 1953, cover an area from Scolt Head on one side of the Wash to Gibraltar Point on the other.

Recovery rates of ringed birds are often very low. But members of the Wash Wader Ringing Group have obtained encouraging results by visiting other countries to study the migratory habits of birds passing through the Wash and other parts of Britain. In recent years their expeditions to Iceland 'controlled' (captured and subsequently released) a good number of British-ringed knots. Many ringed birds are not recovered until killed by trappers or sportsmen. For example, two knots ringed as adults at Snettisham, Norfolk, one in March 1971, the other a year later, were killed at Christchurch, Barbados, West Indies (August 1971) and Broughton Island, Baffin Island, Canada (June 1972) respectively.

Norfolk-ringed knots have also been recovered in France and Poland, while a knot ringed in the Netherlands on 30.3.1968 was controlled in Norfolk at North Wootton (27.8.1968) and Heacham (26.10.1968) before being killed in France on 15.8.1969. A knot ringed in Iceland on 27.5.1957 was seen at Snettisham, Norfolk, on 3.9.1967.

Ringing Reports contain a mass of data relating to many other birds mentioned in this chapter, and a fascinating, even thrilling, experience awaits the naturalist who is prepared to use a good atlas and a little imagination while reading through them.

The hedgehog has a long history as a member of the East Anglian fauna, and ancient records bear witness to its destruction by our forbears. Now one of the region's most widespread mammals, its corpses are still found on gamekeepers' gibbets in Breckland and elsewhere. Hundreds of hedgehogs are killed on the roads each year and many others drown in smooth-sided garden ponds, become entangled in tennis nets, or fall through cattle grids – to mention just some of the hazards besetting these animals. But one must record, with gratitude, that there are people, in town and country alike, prepared to encourage hedgehogs to seek sanctuary in gardens by providing food, often in the form of bread-and-milk, and by leaving bushy untidied corners where breeding or hibernation may take place.

East Anglian hedgehogs hibernate in winter, but may become active during mild spells, especially in places where food is put out for them. Hibernation ends during March and the first litters of 4–5 young are born in May in nests of dry leaves and grasses in hedgerow bottoms, hollows and under cover of low vegetation. Born blind and with the spines sunk in the skin, young hedgehogs have a keen sense of smell and are able to walk soon after birth. Having grown rapidly while being suckled by the mother, the litter disperses, each young hedgehog going its own way, at the age of about six weeks.

The hedgehog's diet has given rise to controversy. A study of individuals trapped on East Anglian estates in summer showed that 20 % of the

Insectivores

Hedgehog

A hedgehog comes out to feed at dusk.

food consisted of earthworms, slugs and snails, and about 70% various insects, mainly beetles. Of 106 stomachs examined 14 contained fragments of egg shells, 12 contained mammal remains (mainly rabbit), and 19 feathers. The fact that hedgehogs *will* take eggs may provide grounds for controlling them on partridge beats. Elsewhere, as pointed out in *Predatory Mammals in Britain*, there is normally no need for control.

Though mainly nocturnal, hedgehogs are occasionally seen during daylight hours. They live in copses, hedgerows, woodland edges, farmland, gardens, churchyards and cemeteries. As a rule, they do not favour Broadland marshes.

Like the hedgehog, the mole has survived centuries of persecution and one still sees lines of hundreds of corpses on fences in East Anglia. True, mole hills can be a nuisance in pastureland and lawns, and moles may disturb seedlings of crop-plants, including forest trees, causing them to wilt. But far more thought should be given to individual cases involving alleged damage by moles before control measures involving that extremely dangerous poison, strychnine, are authorised.

Mole

I must confess that I did not at first take *Predatory Mammals in Britain* seriously when it spoke of moles occasionally damaging shooting interests by tunnelling under partridge nests and causing birds to desert. But I have since learned that this does, in fact, happen, and not only in the case of partridges. A pair of East Anglian stone curlews deserted after a mole had burrowed under and disrupted the nest contents.

The mole spends the greatest part of its life in tunnels underground where it eats large numbers of earthworms, especially in winter, also taking insect larvae, slugs, centipedes, millipedes and vegetable matter. But the quiet and observant rambler is bound, sooner or later, to encounter it on the surface. He will then have an opportunity to notice the animal's fore-limbs with their strong enlarged claws modified for digging, the small stumpy tail tipped with sensitive hairs, and its velvety fur. This fur is normally black but several variant forms also occur in East Anglia, white, cream, orange-coloured, silver-grey, and chocolate brown individuals being among those recorded. He may also share the good fortune of the naturalist who watched a mole turning over small stones as it foraged in shallow water at the edge of a Norfolk stream.

Ordinary mole-hills, heaps of waste earth pushed out by excavating moles, show the course of underground burrows. Fortresses, bigger mounds of earth than ordinary mole-hills, indicate the position of nests of dead leaves and grass, nests used in winter being under larger fortresses than those used by breeding females. In East Anglia mole fortresses are often thrown up beneath bushes or trees, but they also occur in open fields, on the higher, better drained parts of river banks and

Common shrew with an earthworm.

dykes and even on large tussock sedges in Broadland. Movements of moles, sometimes on a large scale, are noticed in the area as, for example, when they leave low-lying water meadows for drier land in winter, and also when they move into marshes and reedbeds during times of low rainfall.

Moles are attacked by several predators, being particularly vulnerable when they appear above ground and when they travel along shallow burrows. Herons are keen mole-hunters, as is evident from the fact that most of the pellets ejected by these birds at three East Anglian heronries contained mole toenails and hair. Mole remains have also been found in pellets from tawny owls and from white storks on Halvergate marshes (See p. 69). Stoats have been seen carrying moles, and cats catch, but do not usually eat, them.

Cats also account for many shrews, a Broadland cat having caught common, pygmy and water shrews one year. Examination of these birds' pellets shows that both barn and tawny owls take shrews in East Anglia and kestrels also prey on them here. Discarded tins and bottles take another heavy toll of shrews (and other small mammals), which, having entered them without difficulty, often find escape impossible. And, of course, shrews are among the numerous creatures killed on the roads. Despite these checks on its numbers, the common shrew is recorded throughout the area, and (like the pygmy shrew) has even been observed on the dunes at Scolt Head Island on occasion. Living in runways in and beneath thick grass and other low vegetation, the ranny (to use a local name) occurs in many different habitats. It enters houses and has even been trapped in upstairs rooms.

The year's adult generation dies in late summer or autumn (some

Shrews

This water shrew is seen with an earthworm, but the species will also tackle bigger animals.

individuals have still been active in Norfolk as late as November), the species being carried through the winter by the year's new generation. During this brief life the shrew is very active, much of its time being spent in seeking food – beetles, earthworms, woodlice, grasshoppers, spiders and fresh carrion – whose daily weight amounts to three-quarters of the animal's own weight (even more in the case of lactating females).

Like the common shrew, the pygmy shrew, our smallest non-flying mammal, lives among ground vegetation in several types of habitat and it, too, enters houses. Water shrews do not make a habit of visiting houses, but one was trapped in a Norfolk apple store in January. Generally they are creatures of rivers, streams, lakes, ponds, dykes, marshes and reedswamps, though they have also been found some distance from water. In many parts of East Anglia quiet observers will find opportunities of watching water shrews swimming and diving and may even see them catching and feeding on freshwater shrimps and snails and water beetles. Water shrews will also tackle bigger animals, attacks on frogs having been seen.

Bats

East Anglian bats take nothing larger than insects and spiders, using echolocation to detect them and to move about without colliding with objects in their line of flight. Some ten species of bats have been recorded from the region, though several are by no means common or widespread. As is the case with so many wild creatures (and plants), one cannot be complacent over the future of even the commoner species. For bats are killed by cars on the roads, by cats and owls. And these harmless creatures also suffer from cleaning operations in churches and house-roofs, while favoured sites are destroyed by clearance of hollow trees and filling in of chalk-pits. Much of this unnecessary suffering and destruction would be avoided if more people read the leaflet *Focus on bats*, an illustrated guide to the conservation and control of bats issued by the Society for the Promotion of Nature Reserves.

Fortunately we have in East Anglia a number of enlightened folk who *are* prepared to help conserve bats and their roosts. For example, Horringer caves, the habitat of five species of bats, are owned by a family who, by their co-operation with the Suffolk Trust for Nature Conservation, deserve our gratitude. So, too, do the conservation work-parties whose strenuous efforts led to the re-opening (after four years) of Eaton chalk caves in 1972 and the erection of a padlocked iron grille to control human access. This old chalk working had been well-known as a winter roost of Daubenton's bats, and it is pleasing to know that at least two were present there only four months after the re-opening.

Daubenton's bats also hibernate in chalk caves near Bury St Edmunds and in a Norfolk icehouse and tunnel. In summer they roost in trees and buildings, including mills on the lower Bure marshes, and feed on small aquatic insects while flying low over water – rivers, lakes and broads (It must not be assumed that Daubenton's bats are the only small bats to fly in this situation: pipistrelles also fly low over water). In 1967 a male Daubenton's was examined in Suffolk 18 years 2 days after being ringed, a longevity record for this species.

Records for age and movement were created by a pipistrelle caught by a cat at Buxton, Norfolk, in October 1969. Over eleven years old, it had moved 43 miles from Bury St Edmunds, Suffolk, where it had been ringed as an adult in 1958. Common and widely distributed, pipistrelles roost in buildings and trees. Their evening flight is generally seen from March until October but it may occur as late as November or December. On several occasions East Anglian pipistrelles have been observed in daylight in winter, even in bitter weather in January and February.

Pipistrelles seem to attract most attention during the three months June to August. This is when pregnant females congregate in large numbers in 'maternity colonies' in churches and other buildings, small gaps being large enough to serve as entrances. Fairly new houses and bungalows are among buildings used by nursing females, the cavity wall of one such place on the edge of the Waveney marshes having sheltered several hundreds. Pipistrelle remains have been found in owl pellets and this, our smallest, bat is sometimes numbered among road casualties.

Noctule bats are not as common as pipistrelles in East Anglia. But there are several places where they occupy summer roosts in hollow trees, old woodpecker holes and cracks in large branches. Noctules are fond of foraging over rubbish tips in search of flying house-crickets. Normally they hawk their prey at tree-top height. On fine summer evenings they fly amongst and about the branches of trees, catching cockchafers, large reddish-brown beetles whose swarms make a loud humming sound. Other large beetles, summer chafers – the 'blind bees' of Norfolk, bring noctules down to hedge level where these insects are taken as they fly away from the foliage. In attempts to discover more about their habits and movements, noctules have been ringed by several East Anglian naturalists. One of these ringed individuals was eaten by a tawny owl, its aluminium ring being found in one of the bird's pellets at Westleton, Suffolk, nearly four years after it had been ringed there.

Like noctules, serotine bats fly low to take summer chafers as they leave roadside hedges. The two species do, in fact, feed and fly together at such times, crossing roads at heights of only a few feet but always managing to avoid traffic. Serotines eat other insects, too, and may be observed taking moths near trees, sometimes right in amongst the branches, and feeding over rubbish dumps. Roosting in buildings in summer, serotines are found under the roof-tiles of Suffolk cottages. They do not seem to have ventured far into Norfolk, though dead specimens have been found in the Yarmouth area.

Common long-eared bats live in both East Anglian counties, roosting in buildings in summer and in churches and other buildings and the Suffolk chalk caves in winter. In summer they are seen hovering round trees as they take moths and other insects from leaves. Common long-eared bats are killed by tawny owls and cats and traffic also takes its toll. (The rare grey long-eared bat has yet to be detected in East Anglia and is at present confined to the south coast of England).

In East Anglia common long-eared bats have been found sharing winter roosts with Daubenton's, already mentioned, and Natterer's bats. The last-named species has been reported from an icehouse, churches, chalk caves and hollow trees in this area.

The whiskered bat, an uncommon species in East Anglia, is particularly fond of spiders and hunts them along fences. It winters in chalk caves in Suffolk and also in old chalk workings at Grime's Graves, an ancient flint-mining site at Weeting, Norfolk.

An elusive species, the Barbastelle bat is rarely seen, but several dead specimens have been found in the region in recent years. A lesser horseshoe bat was seen in a Suffolk chalk cave in 1958 and there is a much older Norfolk record for the species. The parti-coloured bat discovered in a timber yard at Great Yarmouth docks in 1968 may well have been imported with Baltic timber.

I cannot close this section without mentioning the demolition in Suffolk by the Earl of Cranbrook of the ancient belief that women's hair has such strong attractions for bats that, on coming into contact with it, they become inextricably entangled. The Earl, a distinguished student of mammals, used six species of bats, a brunette and three blondes, short and long hair, curly and wavy hair, in his experiments! Not one of the bats became entangled, they walked about on the head and took flight without difficulty.

Sad to say, bats are really well-known to a comparatively few specialists. This cannot be said of the rabbit, for, even in areas where the wild animal is scarce, most people are familiar with one or more of the domestic breeds which arose from it. Rabbits were introduced into Britain by the Normans as a source of meat and fur. Over the centuries they became very common indeed, the British rabbit population being estimated at between 60 million and 100 million before the arrival of myxomatosis in 1953–4.

East Anglia was one of the many areas holding large numbers of rabbits. A large part of Breckland was a real stronghold for them, much of it being covered by warrens where rabbit farming was carried on. Then, in the 1920s, large-scale afforestation commenced there and the status of rabbits began to change from that of a crop to that of a pest. The rabbit was no longer king and 82,312 of them were taken from one area of 6,000 acres after it was enclosed for tree-planting.

Here, and in other parts of East Anglia, the ecological and economic importance of rabbits has been clearly established. By nibbling seedlings and stripping saplings of their bark, rabbits often destroyed them. This helps to prevent natural regeneration of trees and shrubs, and puts the forester to the expense of erecting rabbit-proof fencing and of controlling rabbits. In hard weather rabbits damage older trees, too, by gnawing bark. Field and garden crops are eaten on a large-scale, it having been estimated in one survey of East Anglia in 1949 and 1950 that £100,000 worth of winter corn was lost. Vegetation is greatly affected by grazing rabbits (and, of course, by other grazing animals), grass being reduced to close-cropped turf and sometimes completely destroyed, heather bushes being modified to rounded cushions and often eventually dying. Rabbits did, in fact, contribute to the formation of the grass heath habitat by suppressing the otherwise dominant heather and woodland species.

Although some plants are destroyed by rabbits, their grazing and burrowing, others (for example, certain annuals) are able to grow in the conditions they create. The burrowing of rabbits, especially in light soils in exposed areas, may assist the process of soil erosion, if only in a minor way. On the other hand, conservationists might point to the fact that deserted rabbit burrows may be used as nesting sites by wheatears and shelducks.

During the early 1950s the virus *Myxomatosis cuniculus* spread rapidly through East Anglia, killing vast numbers of rabbits, totally exterminating them in some places. Transmitted mainly by rabbit fleas, it is also carried by mosquitoes, several species of which feed on rabbits. A few rabbits did survive the original epidemic and bred normally, but the disease became endemic among them. In recent years, with their mild winters, rabbits have increased in numbers and are thought by some naturalists to be showing a growing resistance to myxomatosis. Already this revival of rabbit populations is illustrating the complexity of relationships between species and also of problems facing conservationists. Wheatears, stone curlews and lapwings are enjoying the open conditions created by the heavy grazing of rabbits kept in the enclosure at Weeting Heath National Nature Reserve. But elsewhere in Breckland rabbits burrowed under wire netting enclosures protecting plants of spiked speedwell, a very rare Breckland speciality, stripping them of their flowers.

Hares

Correlated with the almost complete extermination of rabbits by myxomatosis was a marked increase in the population of the brown hare and the movement of this species into previously unoccupied, or rarely visited, areas. Nowadays the hare population of East Anglia fluctuates, but not apparently according to any uniform pattern.

Like rabbits, hares are capable of great damage to farming and forestry, especially in hard weather when crops come under particularly heavy attack and bark is gnawed from trees. In some parts of East Anglia hares tend to move into woods in winter. But generally they are creatures of open country, fields and grazing marshes being favoured habitats. Hares also occur at the coast. Blakeney Point has its hares, though they receive sharp treatment from terns when venturing too close to their nests. The hare has been seen on Scolt Head Island, Norfolk, and many have been tagged on the shingle of Orford Beach, the peninsular part of the Orfordness-Havergate National Nature Reserve (Suffolk). Hares visit saltings and on occasion may even be seen running through shallow sea-water. They often swim across marshland dykes, though one Norfolk hare was seen to jump about 8 feet across one. In farming areas hares are best observed with binoculars before crops grow to any height, the 'boxing' displays of so-called 'mad March' hares being seen early in the year. Colour variants of the hare seen in East Anglia include pure white, black, and silver-grey and white individuals.

Rodents

Squirrels

The black form of our next species, the red squirrel, is seen in the region on occasion, but albinos of this species are very rare. Red squirrels are widespread in East Anglia and in places quite abundant, despite recent outbreaks of 'red squirrel disease'. They live in coniferous and mixed woods and belts of trees, feeding on seeds of pine and other trees, buds, berries and fungi. They also take insects and the eggs and nestlings of birds. Their habit of eating the bark off the leading shoots

A red squirrel at a water tank in Rendlesham Forest, Suffolk. The characteristic ear-tufts are clearly seen.

of conifers, ruining them for the production of straight timber, has led to control measures being applied against them at times.

Red squirrels are sometimes seen searching for scraps in lay-bys, and they will visit gardens to feed at bird-tables and also from dust-bins. They may even find their way into houses (one Suffolk red squirrel used to enter through a ventilator). Red squirrels are known to gnaw bones and this was undoubtedly why gnawed bones of pig's trotters were found in an East Anglian drey (nest) and why on another occasion a red squirrel was seen carrying a tooth-marked bone.

There is no true hibernation in this species. Wintry conditions are said to inhibit activity, but 25 years ago I used to see red squirrels scratching about under a large beech at Old Buckenham on cold frosty January and February mornings. True, there were mornings when I did not see them and they were probably sheltering within the shredded bark lining of their spherical dreys.

Many years ago East Anglians observed the custom of hunting red squirrels on Christmas morning. Nowadays their hunting is directed against the introduced American grey squirrel. The practice of releasing these animals in English woods had become something of a fashion by 1889, and at about that time an attempted introduction of grey squirrels at Northrepps, Norfolk, failed after a preliminary success. Elsewhere introductions were successful, but grey squirrels were not noticed in East Anglia until a few individuals turned up in east Suffolk during the early 1930s. By 1955–56 the species had penetrated west Suffolk. In 1963 the first pairs moved into Norfolk, and since then grey squirrels have spread over much of the southern half of the county and into parts of central and northern Norfolk too. Shooting and trapping are now being employed against them in East Anglia, and many corpses are displayed on gamekeepers' gibbets.

This mammal, the grey squirrel, lacks ear-tufts. An introduced species, it has become a serious pest.

This increase of grey squirrels, which have already caused much damage to sycamore, beech and other broadleaved trees, comes at a time when the range of the red squirrel is contracting. It is therefore encouraging to know that the Forestry Commission has set aside two large blocks of Breckland forest specifically for the conservation of the red squirrel.

Rats

Like the grey squirrel, the brown rat is both a pest and an introduced species (It arrived in Britain early in the 18th century). And, despite all efforts to eliminate it, it is still seen in many parts of East Anglia. Brown rats eat vast quantities of grain and other food intended for man and his domesticated livestock and spoil large amounts, too. They also affect man's interests by carrying the disease organisms of food poisoning (*Salmonella*), trichinosis and leptospiral jaundice. Fortunately they have many enemies besides man. In East Anglia bones of brown rats are commonly found in barn owl pellets, especially near houses and farm buildings and in arable farming districts, and they also occur in tawny owl pellets. The food of short-eared owls includes many brown rats, as does that of kestrels, foxes, stoats and weasels.

As killers, or destroyers, brown rats themselves can have a considerable effect on other creatures. Regarded as deadly enemies of game, they also kill and eat poultry and other birds and destroy many eggs. On the north Norfolk coastal marshes and Breydon mudflats brown rats live on shellfish and small crabs (and anything else that is edible!) while at Brinton, Norfolk, they have been known to kill and eat large numbers of spawning toads. In East Anglia frogs, snails, house mice and freshwater mussels have also formed part of the diet of hungry rats. Not that they avoid plant foods! In addition to grain, mentioned

Adult and young of the wood mouse, a common and widely distributed East Anglian mammal.

earlier, seeds of wild plants are eaten. Several kinds of fruit were taken during a recent dry summer when several observers saw rats climbing bushes and trees in search of them. In Broadland rats gnaw rhizomes and shoots of reeds in winter, and in Breckland fields carrots are consumed. Eating, as they do, such a great variety of foods, it is not surprising that brown rats can live almost anywhere.

Mice

Like brown rats in certain parts of East Anglia, which have shown resistance to this poison, house mice in the region have been eating warfarin without apparent ill-effects, even chewing through bags to get at it. Largely ignored by naturalists, house mice still live in houses, gardens and garden sheds in various parts of East Anglia where their remains are occasionally found in owl pellets. A few years ago, while living at Stoke-by-Clare, Suffolk, I trapped very few of them in the house. But I caught several specimens of the yellow-necked mouse in the same building. This species is plentiful in parts of Suffolk but rarely recorded in Norfolk. It occurs in woods, hedgerows, gardens (where it can be a nuisance in summer), greenhouses and outbuildings. Some scientists have considered that there is no specific difference between the yellow-necked mouse and the wood mouse (also called long-tailed field mouse). But, be that as it may, the wood mouse is common and widely distributed in East Anglia.

In summer wood mice live in similar places to those listed for yellow-necked mice, and they have also been found in Broadland carrs, and on Breckland heaths, Blakeney Point sand dunes and, very rarely, on Scolt Head Island. Wood mice often enter buildings in winter, but many of them survive under the protective covering of snow, moving about safely out of reach of predators. In Norfolk they lived in a caravan, building their winter nests there.

A harvest mouse at its nest in a reedbed.

Generally most active at night, wood mice may sometimes be observed in broad daylight as they feed or collect nesting material. But the naturalist may have to be content with evidence of their presence in the form of food-stores in old birds' nests (one contained 250 haws, 70 hips and other seeds). Food for winter use is often stored underground where nests of finely shredded grass are made. But, as already mentioned, some wood mice make their winter quarters elsewhere, even nest-boxes on tree-trunks, at heights of up to 10 feet from the ground, being used for this purpose. One Suffolk pair had stored 109 conkers (horse chestnut seeds) in such a box.

Wood mice eat many kinds of seeds, including peanuts, sometimes taken from bird tables and feeding trays in gardens. Their habit of venturing into fields, often well away from woods, hedges and other cover, to feed on sugar beet seeds has been causing some concern in spring. The mouse locates each seed accurately, digs it up and then extracts and consumes the embryo. This species is also known to graze down sprouting winter wheat, while gardeners have noted its fondness for newly-sown peas, crocus corms, tulip shoots, and buds and flowers of the Christmas rose. Soap and wallpaper, too, have been consumed by wood mice, and in winter they have been seen in daylight stripping bark from woodland shrubs. Wood mice are taken by cats, barn and tawny owls, and other predators, many die on the roads, and others are trapped in empty bottles.

In East Anglia cats and barn owls are among the predators of the harvest mouse whose nests were once common in cornfields but are now more likely to be found without too much difficulty on rough marshes and river banks, in reedbeds, and in coarse vegetation of undisturbed corners of Broadland and the coastal belt. Dahlia beds and rough parts of large gardens have also proved suitable to this tiny, dainty species, and in winter nests are built in temporary reed stacks in Broadland. The distribution of the 'ginger mouse', as the harvest mouse is called on the north Norfolk coast, appears to have been affected by changing farming and harvesting methods, as noted by East Anglian naturalists in the 1930s. The old-time reaper could, if he so desired, spare the nests of birds and mammals that lay in the path of his sickle. The driver of a modern farm machine works at a much greater speed and is not always able to take such personal decisions. Certainly we must retain some rough unkept areas where quiet observers may still enjoy the pleasure of watching the harvest mouse running up plant stalks and using its long, prehensile tail as a 'fifth hand'.

The dormouse, another attractive little animal, is very rare in East Anglia, being confined to the Stour valley in Suffolk. Dormice from Surrey were introduced into south-east Norfolk in 1844, but the species has not been recorded there in recent years.

Voles

Bank voles are common and widespread in the region, gardens, woods, hedges, river banks and grassland being among their habitats. They enter buildings, including apple stores, especially in autumn and winter. In gardens bank voles can be a nuisance, for they eat bulbs and crocus corms. Insects, both adult forms and larvae, are also taken by bank voles, as Mr. W. H. Payn, the distinguished Suffolk ornithologist, discovered when maggots intended as food for his birds disappeared daily from the tin in which he kept them.

More of a pest than the last species, the short-tailed field vole is the most important prey item of East Anglian barn owls, and tawny owls also take it here. Short-eared owls and kestrels are quick to appear on marshes and other open grassland where field voles have increased in numbers as part of the species' four-yearly cycle of abundance and decline. But their attacks are not believed to have much effect on the vole's numbers. Herons, cats and dogs, and stoats and weasels also account for many field voles, and others are found dead in bottles and on the roads.

This water vole has returned to her disturbed nest to care for six young born only a few hours previously.

Generally considered to feed mainly on grass, field voles are said to have ring-barked and killed over half a pine plantation in Norfolk. Their main breeding season is from March to September, but in Broadland young have been born as late as December. Nests, usually of grass, are often made amongst grass tussocks, but they have been discovered in heaps of garden refuse and in an old black-headed gull's nest. Unlike bank voles, field voles are not noted as climbers, but their ability as swimmers must enable some at least to survive flooding of low-lying land. In East Anglia they have been seen swimming across ponds and between grass tussocks on flooded marshes. But in Broadland they are known to perish in tidal floods.

An expert swimmer and diver, the water vole is sometimes called 'water rat', a misleading name which may unfortunately encourage people to attack it. Living along banks of rivers, streams and dykes (including brackish ones on coastal marshes) in many parts of the region, the water vole may occasionally be found in field pits and garden ponds a mile or two from running water. Both the normal dark brown form of this species and its black colour variant occur in East Anglia. Water voles eat a variety of vegetable matter. Marsh marigold, yellow flag, reedmace and reed sweet-grass are among foodplants of this species in East Anglia. Water voles have been observed eating bark off roots of apple and pear trees in Norfolk, while in Suffolk they have killed young poplar trees by devouring the roots and young larches by eating the bark. One was seen to climb into the upper branches of a hawthorn and feed on newly-opened leaf buds, and another to climb into a field maple bush and eat the leaves. In East Anglia the water vole also eats pond snails, sometimes sitting on a branch overhanging the water while doing so. The hunched-up attitude assumed as it sits holding the food with its forelimbs is characteristic of the species.

East Anglian rivers and broads are ideal feeding and breeding grounds for this animal, the coypu.

Water voles have many enemies, including barn and tawny owls, the heron, bittern, stoat and pike. They also suffer from disturbance of various kinds. Modification of habitats by coypus has, in fact, been suggested as one possible reason for the absence of water voles in parts of East Anglia.

The coypu is a native of South America where it lives as a semi-aquatic animal in and around swamps, lakes and rivers. Its soft dense under-fur is the greyish brown 'nutria' of commerce. Demand for the pelts encouraged fur-farmers to import coypus during the inter-war years and eventually some fifty British farms raised them. Being able to climb wire netting as high as eight feet, to burrow long distances into banks, and to bite its way through wire netting with its powerful teeth, the coypu proved to be a great escaper. By 1937 several coypus were loose in Norfolk and others are said to have been released from captivity early in the war. The county's rivers and broads proved to be ideal for both feeding and breeding, and small feral populations of coypus were established there by the early 1940s. Organised trapping having failed to eliminate them, coypus soon spread into Suffolk.

Coypu

By the mid-1950s the coypu population was not only large but expanding. Then, in 1962, the coypu was recognised as a pest and added to the list of species included in the Destructive Imported Animals Act. Assisted by the severe winter of 1962–63, which killed 80–90% of the coypu population, an official campaign ran from 1962 to late 1965. Numbers were drastically reduced and survivors confined to the Norfolk Broads and certain other areas where complete extermination of the species was thought to be impossible. 'Coypu Control' is still active in East Anglia where 3,252 of the animals were killed in 1972, leaving a population estimated at between 8,000 and 11,000.

Female coypus breed continuously from the age of 3–7 months,

Right This sugar beet crop was badly damaged by coypus.

Below Shells of freshwater mussels showing the effects of predation by coypus.

producing about five offspring in a litter. The young are suckled for the first 6–7 weeks of their lives, but they are eating a lot of adult food by the time they are 2–3 weeks old. Although they sometimes eat freshwater mussels, the food of coypus is mainly vegetable matter. When they abounded in Broadland these selective feeders caused some marked changes in the vegetation. Many reedbeds, particularly those fringing broads and rivers, were completely destroyed, the young shoots, leaves and rhizomes of reeds being devoured in large quantities. In places reeds were replaced by rond-grass, a species better able to withstand the attacks of coypus.

Beds of both greater and lesser reedmace were cleared and even seedlings destroyed. Water lilies, great water dock, meadowsweet, fen rush and great hairy willowherb were among many other species destroyed or damaged. Purple loosestrife, sweet flag and other plants grew in places cleared by coypus, and wading birds found newly exposed areas of mud in which to probe. Elsewhere coypus have been seen feeding on beach refuse on the Norfolk coast. In raids on gardens on the outskirts of Norwich they devoured parsnip tops and sprouts. Sugar beet and corn crops have also been attacked.

Apart from man, coypus have few serious enemies in Britain. Herons, bitterns and birds of prey have been known to make occasional attacks on the young, as have stoats and foxes, two species discussed in the next section.

Carnivores

Fox

Despite the fact that farmers and gamekeepers exercise heavy control against them in many parts of East Anglia, foxes are common in some places and have indeed increased here in recent years. Individuals may be seen during the hours of daylight and also in car headlights, and they

The fox whose mixed diet includes ground-nesting birds, poultry and lambs.

can be tracked in snow and also by smell! The history of the fox in the region is complicated, for, at times, it appears to have been protected for hunting and individuals have been introduced for this purpose.

The case against the fox is based on its destruction of ground-nesting birds (game birds included), poultry and lambs. But it is important to remember that its diet also includes hares, rabbits (an important item before myxomatosis), field voles, fruit and insects. By using a spot-light, a Norfolk observer discovered that this last type of food included large moths, which were caught in flight. Examination of stomach contents has shown that East Anglian foxes also feed on earthworms and several species of fungi. Bones and remains left near fox-earths have provided further evidence of Reynard's feeding habits. At one East Anglian earth there were carcases of woodpigeons, moles, newborn roe kids, rabbits and pheasants.

A fact which surprises many people is that several of these prey-species associate, apparently without fear, with foxes when these carnivores are not actually hunting. Thus pheasants will follow a rooting fox, picking up food from the disturbed earth, and they will even relax with the animal while it sunbathes.

Foxes naturally take advantage of the cover provided by scrub and woodlands, especially young plantations, but they also inhabit East Anglian marshlands where conditions are very open. They are likely to turn up in almost any part of the region, having been seen in Norwich and other towns, on Blakeney Point and in Broadland, where foxes were formerly absent, in recent years.

Control measures against foxes sometimes result in badgers being destroyed in East Anglia, as when badger setts are mistaken for fox

Badger

117

A badger leaves its sett at dusk.

earths during gassing operations. Again, badgers may perish in fox snares. This is a very sad state of affairs because badgers are very far from being plentiful in the region, and have suffered much persecution there in recent times. Certain landowners and gamekeepers *are* interested in having badgers on their land and some small-scale attempts to re-introduce them have been made. The Forestry Commission has encouraged badgers by providing badger gates in their boundary fences.

In East Anglia badger setts occur mainly in coniferous and deciduous woods and on heathland. Some are excavated on slopes, but others in flat ground. The earthworks of the setts often attract attention, but the surrounding ground is clean and tidy (Badgers even dig and use special dung-pits). The naturalist who is allowed to visit an East Anglian sett, and to observe the occupants as they emerge at dusk, should count himself fortunate and keep the exact location to himself.

Many of the complaints against badgers are imaginary or arise through ignorance of their feeding habits. In most of Britain, badgers in moderate numbers do little harm and quite a lot of good, and only under exceptional circumstances do they need controlling. True, badgers do occasionally eat pheasant and partridge eggs but not enough to cause significant losses. In East Anglia, in fact, pheasants are known to have hatched out their full clutches within a few yards of badger setts. Normally badgers do not kill poultry, and losses caused through their rolling in corn and eating grain are, as a rule, insignificant. Badgers eat a large variety of animal and vegetable foods, including young rabbits, mice, rats, snails, wasp grubs, fruit, fungi and grass. But earthworms form the most important single item of their diet, and in autumn acorns are taken whenever they are available.

Otter

Like the badger, the otter is an endangered species in East Anglia and it is therefore encouraging to find protection being given to it in a few places. One hopes that such protection will be extended to other areas and that it will prove possible to enforce it.

Otters are usually nocturnal, resting during the day in burrows, drains and other sheltered places, and so it is not surprising that reports of their occurrence are often based on the presence of 'spraints' (droppings), 'seals' (footprints), and remains of otter meals.

Examination of spraints and remains of otter meals in north Norfolk led scientists to conclude that 3-spined sticklebacks and eels constituted the bulk of the otter's diet in the area. Trout bones were present in the spraints on one occasion only, despite the fact that these fish are fairly common in local rivers. Roach, rudd, perch, crayfish and moorhens were among other creatures taken by these Norfolk otters.

Like spraints and seals, slides on steep river banks, and those in snow, tell something of the movements and habits of otters. Their tobogganing down these slides is a form of play and so is the frolicking with eels enjoyed by young otters before they actually eat their prey.

Stoat

Stoats often play together, leaping, chasing, boxing and wrestling, and individuals, too, perform curious antics. These small carnivores are frequent in many parts of East Anglia where corpses often appear on gamekeepers' gibbets. Such action against stoats can, in certain circumstances, be short-sighted. Individuals do take adults, eggs and chicks of poultry, game and other birds. But the species as a whole destroys large numbers of rabbits (its most important food before myxomatosis), rats, mice and voles. There have been one or two cases of stoats living in or near terneries on both Blakeney Point and Scolt Head Island and feeding only or mainly on rabbits. On the other hand, there have been times when stoats, having played havoc with nests and chicks of terns and black-headed gulls, had to be controlled at these reserves.

In addition to coastal dunes, stoats inhabit woods, marshes, Broadland carrs and reedswamps, and farmland. Observers may find them hunting in the open (they are active day and night) or feeding on corpses of creatures killed on the roads. On occasion they may be seen swimming across rivers or running along the branches of trees high above the ground.

These stoats were destroyed by a gamekeeper, but such action is sometimes short-sighted.

In recent winters there have been several reports of East Anglian stoats in 'ermine', their coats, brown during the rest of the year, being white except for the black tip of the tail. Other individuals have gone partially into 'ermine'. White stoats are, of course, far more plentiful in northern counties.

Weasel

White forms of the weasel are very rare in Britain. Closely related to the stoat, but a much smaller animal, the weasel is abundant and widespread in East Anglia. Woodland, farmland, hedgerows, Broadland carrs

A weasel drags away a vole, one of several small mammals taken as prey.

and marshes are among the habitats of the mouse-hunt (to use a local name), individuals of which have ventured into the centre of Norwich, King's Lynn and other East Anglian towns.

Apart from voles and mice, weasels destroy such other small mammals as shrews, moles and rats. Small birds, too, fall victim to weasels, which do not hesitate to eat the remains of sparrows and other creatures killed on the roads. The fact that they take game chicks occasionally results in weasels being destroyed on some estates, though, taking a wider view, they are friends of farmers and gamekeepers alike. Being small creatures, weasels are able to hunt through stacks of straw bales, mouse and vole burrows, and mole runs.

Weasels are known to fight one another and to show considerable aggression in capitivity. But they are nevertheless beset by enemies, including, as we have already noted, man. Cats hunt and kill them, their remains occur in owl pellets, and on the roads traffic takes its toll. But the weasel's life is not a ceaseless round of hunting and being hunted, a fact that becomes evident when one meets a family party moving about the countryside. For a time, it is true, the animals move in line, but soon they pause to play, rolling in a bundle and jumping on one another. Weasels readily take to water, but they are not such practised climbers as stoats.

American mink

The American mink, a relation of stoat and weasel, climbs well and is an excellent swimmer, some of its food being caught in water. Introduced into Britain in 1929, it was not long before individuals escaped from fur farms and dispersed into the wild. Soon American mink began to be reported from Broadland, Breckland, the coastal region and other parts of East Anglia and several were captured. One caught at Wroxham had lived in the thatch of a cottage, feeding on fish from the broad, while

Otter. This is an endangered species in East Anglia, but there are places where otters may still be seen at play like those in this picture.

during the same year, 1970, twelve were trapped at Welney Wildfowl Reserve. The classification of the American mink as a potentially very destructive predator marked it out for stringent control and very little has been heard of it in the region during the last few years.

Of East Anglian marine mammals, the most familiar is the common seal, large numbers of which breed on the sandbanks of the Wash where hunting of pups under Home Office licence has attracted national attention. There are colonies too, at Blakeney Point and Scroby Sands off Great Yarmouth. From time to time common seals are seen at other places round the coast of the region and occasionally individuals appear inland, having made their way up rivers.

Seals

Some idea of the journeys made by seals can be gained from recoveries of seal pups tagged in the Wash. These have been made along the Suffolk and Essex coasts to the south, the Yorkshire, Durham and East Lothian coasts to the north, and at Dunkirk, Ostend, Wester Schelde, and even further afield. Feeding on fish, shell-fish, shrimps, prawns and crabs, common seals are not always popular with fishermen. In East Anglian waters common seals produce their young during late June and early July. And, unlike grey seal pups, they are able to take to the water within a few hours of their birth, so that sandbanks where breeding females haul out need be uncovered for short periods only.

Common seals did not receive legal protection until the Conservation of Seals Act 1970 came into force. Now a close season operates from June 1 to August 31 and, as already indicated, hunters operate under licence.

The 1970 Act also applies to the grey seal, subject of an earlier Act and, like the common seal, victim of much persecution in the past. This species appears to have bred spasmodically on the Wash sandbanks since about 1880 and it still occurs there, apparently without breeding during recent years. In 1958 breeding of grey seals was confirmed at Scroby Sands off Great Yarmouth, habitat of a herd of common seals. Within eight years, however, the structure of Scroby Sands had changed so that very little, if any, sand was left above water at high tide. Grey seals, whose pups are unable to leave the 'beach' until they are several days old, did not breed there for a year or two. By 1970 Scroby Sands were building up once more and grey seal pups are again being born there from late November to January, several weeks after the species' pupping season has finished in northerly parts of Britain.

Marking has shown that from time to time East Anglian colonies are joined by grey seals from the Farne Islands. Marked at birth in the Farnes, one grey seal was found alive on the beach at Sea Palling, just north of Scroby Sands, two months later and returned to the sea. Another was seen in a distressed condition at Covehithe on the Suffolk coast three months after being ringed as a calf on the Farnes.

Deer   Leaving the flesh-eaters, we reach deer, remembering that the original wild ones of East Anglia were exterminated long ago.

The red deer seen here today may well be descendants of outliers from the Stag Hunt. Great wanderers, they are spreading through woodland in parts of the region. Regular visitors to Breckland stand a good chance of seeing them eventually, as do observers in the country south-west of Halesworth, East Suffolk. One has to remember that normally red deer feed at nightfall and at dawn and that during the day they lie chewing the cud. Grass and young heather shoots are their staple food, but in recent years there have been a few reports of East Anglian red deer damaging young plantations.

In this region roe deer have been seen feeding with red deer stags and travelling through the woods with them. The six pairs of roe from Württemburg, Germany, which were introduced in north-west Suffolk about 1884, increased considerably. Some spread southwards into Suffolk, and others crossed the Little Ouse into Norfolk. Nowadays roe are plentiful throughout the Breckland forests and they are spreading into other areas. The visitor may meet a forester prepared to point out a favourite haunt of roe, perhaps an area of dense undergrowth where both cover and food are available. But the naturalist walking quietly through the forests is likely to catch a glimpse of roe as they graze in the rides or move about. He may disturb roe and see them leap away, showing the conspicuous rump patch, the target, as it is known.

When the animals themselves are out of sight tracks on bare soil and droppings on grass and other vegetation indicate their presence in a district. In spring fraying stocks – small bushes or trees whose stems have been stripped of bark – appear where bucks have cleaned their antlers of velvet and marked their territories with scent secreted from glands in the skin of the forehead. Rutting rings, worn pathways, in the form of circles or figures of eight, appear where bucks chase, or drive, the does during the mating season or rut (late July to August) and the false rut (October or November), and where does and their previous year kids play in spring.

Fraying damages and even destroys trees, while browsing by roe deer may cripple their growth. Grazing by roe may destroy small seedling trees and thus prevent natural regeneration. On the other hand, it may reduce fire hazard by keeping down vegetation on rides and other open spaces in the woods. Roe have been observed grazing winter wheat in the region, but no serious damage appears to have been reported. In East Anglian forests roe are controlled so as to maintain a healthy population at a level which does not involve more damage than can reasonably be tolerated. They are occasionally killed on the faster stretches of road, but reflectors provided on roadside posts often help,

Fallow buck with well-developed, palmated antlers.

by reflecting from headlights into the woods, to keep deer out of harm's way.

Unlike red deer and roe, fallow deer cannot be described as indisputably native to Britain. Certainly they have a long history as park animals, Domesday Book having recorded fallow deer in many such places. Nowadays herds are maintained at Great Witchingham, Melton Constable, Holkham and Houghton in Norfolk, and at Helmingham and Ickworth in Suffolk. Wild herds developed from park escapes exist in wooded areas around Horsford and King's Lynn in Norfolk, and in west, northeast and south Suffolk. At times it has been found necessary to control these animals because of damage done to trees and farm crops. Their food also includes grasses, mosses, nuts and berries. Usually feeding at dusk and dawn along the margins of woods and in neighbouring fields, fallow deer occasionally appear during the day, especially in winter when they may be forced to scrape snow from grass and moss.

There is no doubt whatever about the status of the remaining species of deer seen in East Anglia, for they were all introduced in relatively recent times.

A small relative of the red deer, the sika deer has been seen in the wild in Norfolk on one or two occasions. A herd of this species is maintained at Melton Constable Park.

Photographed in the open, this muntjac had emerged from dense vegetation, its natural habitat.

Originally introduced at Woburn about 1900, the Chinese muntjac is a 'barking-deer', standing barely eighteen inches in height. Widely distributed in East Anglia, it turns up in all sorts of places, including gardens. Spending much of its time in dense undergrowth, in which it uses well-defined runs, and being able to move through standing crops, it attracts little attention. On occasion Chinese muntjac are seen in car headlights or flushed in woods in areas where their presence has not even been suspected. It is possible that they have been confused with the next species, Chinese water deer, in the past.

Standing about twenty inches high at the shoulder, Chinese water deer never carry antlers (muntjac develop short, simple ones), but they display two sharp canine tusks. Introduced into Britain at Woburn about 1900, they have since appeared in private collections in Broadland. Escapes were perhaps inevitable and in 1968 two specimens, one of which later became a road casualty, were seen at Hickling. During the following four years several Chinese water deer have been found dead on roads in Fenland, on the western edge of Norfolk, and in Broadland. Despite these setbacks, there is evidence that this species is living in dense reedbeds in Broadland at Hickling and in several other parishes, and in the coastal belt at Cley. In their native swamps in China, Chinese water deer produce five to six young in a litter. It will be interesting to watch their progress in the wild in East Anglia.

Amphibians and reptiles

As in so many other parts of Britain, amphibians and reptiles do not appear to be as common or as widespread in East Anglia as they were in, say, the 1930s. Various reasons for these changes have been advanced: building development, pollution, fires, floods and drainage all being blamed. But we must not overlook the fact that many people seem to be unable to leave these creatures, particularly snakes and slow-worms, unharmed. And they have enemies other than man to contend with.

Newts

Each of the three British newts is represented here. The palmate newt seems to be confined to the eastern part of the region, the smooth newt and the warty newt being more widely distributed. During the breeding season the smooth newt is common in ponds and ditches where the female lays up to 350 eggs. At other times it lives on land, hiding by day under logs or stones, in cracks in the earth or in thick grass, emerging at night to feed. During hibernation, from late October or November to February or early March, smooth newts may also be found in cellars and garden sheds. Carnivorous in their diet, they take live food only. They themselves have been swallowed by warty newts, but such behaviour is unusual!

The palmate newt may sometimes have been confused with the smooth newt and fresh searches for it should certainly be made. Although it lives at sea level in some parts of the country and has been reliably recorded in East Anglia, the palmate newt appears to be most at home in hilly country.

Unlike the palmate newt, the warty or great crested newt is not a montane species. Living in lakes, ponds and dykes, it is more aquatic in its habits than either of the previous two species, though it usually hibernates on land. Like other newts, the warty newt is a voracious feeder, insect larvae, small crustacea, tadpoles and worms all being taken.

In captivity newts are long-lived, the female warty newt having been known to live for 27 years, the male for 25. But their numerous enemies may well prevent them from reaching such ages in the wild. Tadpoles of newts are devoured by snakes, fish, water-birds and larvae of certain aquatic insects. Some of these creatures take adult newts in water, while hedgehogs, rats and other predators destroy them on land. Smooth and palmate newts are common victims, but the warty newt, whose skin produces a distasteful secretion, is often left alone.

Toads

The common toad is another species whose skin secretion affords it a certain amount of protection against its enemies, though some of them know how to avoid the skin while feeding on the animal's inside. Like the frog, the toad declined over much of England during the 1960s, the garden pond being the only habitat in which it increased. Still widespread in East Anglia, despite their reduced numbers, toads make for their breeding ponds towards the end of March or early April. Many are killed while crossing busy roads, others are devoured at breeding sites by rats, herons and other predators.

After spawning, when eggs are laid in long strings, adult toads disperse into drier areas, the minute young leaving the water eight to twelve weeks later. Toads have large appetites, certain species of beetles and ants forming an important part of their diet. On occasion they may be seen sitting in wait for insects flying to both light and trees 'sugared' by moth-collectors. They will also wait at the entrance of hives, ready to snap up bees that come within reach (32 bees were found in one toad's stomach). Toads usually commence hibernation in disused burrows or other dry sheltered places in October or November. But on October 25, 1945, during a spell of mild weather, H. W. Back, then Honorary Secretary of the Norfolk and Norwich Naturalists' Society, heard toads croaking at Hethersett Hall, near Norwich, and in the third week of November tadpoles were active in the lake there.

Distinguished from the common toad by the yellow stripe down the middle of its back, the natterjack is a much rarer species whose disappearance from many of its former East Anglian haunts has alarmed conservationists. Sandy places with ready access to water are favoured by the running toad – the name refers to the natterjack's manner of movement, it being incapable of hopping because of the shortness of its hind legs.

One naturalist's fieldwork at Winterton Dunes National Nature Reserve on the East Norfolk coast revealed something of the hazards facing natterjacks. Those that spawned in water lying in 'damp slacks', depressions behind the sand-dunes, did so in late April. Unfortunately this was when the water level started to drop steadily, with the result that conditions became unsuitable for tadpoles, which perished. During the three years of the study (1961–63) two batches of toadlets survived on the reserve. One lot, some 20–30, came from spawn deposited in a wartime mortar crater. The other resulted from an experiment in which natterjack tadpoles were introduced into a polythene-lined depression whose water level was kept constant. The toadlets that successfully left the water had survived the attacks of carnivorous beetles, smooth newts and larvae of the great water beetle and the cannibalism of tadpoles of their own species. There was only one successful breeding season during the five years following the study period and that after unusually heavy rainfall in May. Three years saw very few toadlets produced and during the fifth year there was no standing water in April and natterjacks did not assemble for breeding. In recent years conservation measures have been taken at Winterton and at another place in north Norfolk, natterjacks having bred successfully at both sites.

Frogs   Although it is still much more familiar to most people than the last species, the common frog has become scarce in parts of East Anglia and there are places where it has disappeared completely in recent years. Drainage of wetland habitats, filling in of ponds and ditches, insecticides, and pressure of our human population (including its vast intake of frogs for use in biological laboratories) have all contributed to its decline. Then there are major enemies like herons and ringed snakes and others such as ducks, rats and hedgehogs, all ready to seize a creature that lives on worms, slugs, insects and their larvae. One can only appeal to owners of garden ponds to allow frogs to continue to breed there and to provide them with the means of leaving those that are steep-sided.

Ponds form the habitat of the edible frog, a noisy and voracious creature whose adult life, including hibernation, is spent in or beside the water. During the first half of the 19th century several batches of edible frogs were imported from the Continent by a Norfolk landowner who deposited them in ponds, ditches and fens. After having been reported as dispersed and well established, little, if anything, was heard of the species in the county for many years. Then, in 1966, it was rediscovered at three ponds in south-west Norfolk and on 7th August eight years later 42 edible frogs were counted there. One hopes that they and the members of two isolated smaller colonies, which have since been found, will be left to breed, for edible frogs are attractive creatures, especially when basking in the sunshine and showing their beautiful green upper parts.

This is a convenient place, too, to appeal to the clergy and their parishioners to allow wild creatures to continue to live at peace in village churchyards.

Slow-worm

Such places are the only undisturbed habitats left to slow-worms in many areas. Harmless, feeding on worms, slugs, spiders and insects, 'blind-worms' (as slow-worms are also called) also inhabit dry heaths, woods and hedgerows. In early spring and late summer slow-worms may be seen in the daytime, but otherwise they are content to remain in hiding places until dusk. Often regarded as snakes, slow-worms are, in fact, limbless lizards whose highly polished appearance, due to the smoothness of their scales, makes them attractive little animals.

A beautiful colour variety is confined to males. Such blue-spotted slow-worms, with bright blue spots or lines on the upper parts of the body, are seen in East Anglia occasionally and an all-blue male was found in a Broadland churchyard. Slow-worms, especially the worm-like very young ones, have many enemies among birds and mammals, including some that are scarce or protected species.

Lizard

Much more abundant and widespread than the slow-worm, the common or viviparous lizard lives in a wide variety of habitats, including heaths, commons, gardens, banks and sand-dunes. A hardy species, it

This adder displays the characteristic markings of the species, our only venomous snake.

Snakes

may be seen sunning itself in March when the bitter northerly wind is blowing and snow lies under the hedges. Feeding on spiders, insects and their larvae, viviparous lizards are themselves devoured by hedgehogs, pheasants, adders and ringed snakes.

Of the two snakes just mentioned, the adder or viper occurs on dry heaths, coastal dunes, fens and rough ground in East Anglia. It may be seen in such places early in the year when, on emerging from hibernation, it suns itself, sometimes when snow lingers under the hedges. At other times it is not easy to surprise, usually seeking cover at the slightest hint of danger.

In addition to lizards, already mentioned, adders eat voles, mice and other small mammals, slow-worms, frogs, newts and young birds. Yet there is a record of a Suffolk adder, nine inches long, that was killed and gnawed almost in halves by a house mouse with which it was left overnight in a vivarium! Adders themselves are destroyed by man and by the hedgehog, whose spines protect it when, after giving the snake a sudden bite, it quickly curls up, later uncoiling to repeat the attack.

In parts of East Anglia adders are said to have been fairly abundant in many woods before the introduction of pheasants, a fact which is

Edible frog. The rediscovery of this introduced
species in Norfolk in 1966 was a notable event. In
sunshine the upper parts are usually green, but in
captivity and away from the sun this beautiful
colour is soon lost.

A ringed snake basks on a sunny bank.

easier to grasp when one discovers that one of these birds was found to have eight young adders in its crop. Adders, which will deliberately take to water, have also been removed from the stomachs of pike and eels. They are occasionally run over and killed on our roads, too.

A male adder measuring 24 inches is considered well-grown. Although females grow larger than males, not many exceed 27 inches in length. An exceptional specimen, one of $38\frac{1}{2}$ inches containing 20 embryos, was reported from Walberswick, Suffolk, in 1971.

A timid creature, the adder is our only venomous snake, but cases of viper-bite are few and far between in East Anglia. Anyone who is bitten by an adder should be taken quickly but quietly to a doctor.

Unlike the adder, which actually gives birth to its young, the ringed snake (or grass-snake) deposits its eggs in heaps of manure, sawdust, or rotting leaves, where their development is assisted by the warmth generated in such matter. In June or July the female lays from 8 to 40 eggs, the actual number depending on her age, older females producing more than younger ones. The eggs hatch in from 6 to 10 weeks, the tiny snakes going into hiding, where some escape the attentions of their numerous enemies.

Adult ringed snakes prefer sunny places near water, open woods, hedgerows and marshes being well favoured, the last-named especially in summer. They are very fond of frogs and, being good swimmers, often hunt them in ponds. Fish and tadpoles are captured in this way, too. Small birds and mammals are also taken, sometimes on the ground, at other times in bushes and low trees, the ringed snake being a good climber. Although this species is rare in much of Broadland, it inhabits marshes and reedswamps by the rivers Yare and Waveney in spring and summer.

As it is not possible to deal adequately with more than a few of the numerous East Anglian insects here, I propose to devote this limited space to some that are subjects of conservation measures or interesting in other ways. As in other parts of Britain, small tortoiseshells, red admirals and certain other butterflies are attracted to parks and gardens, but many species prefer uncultivated places where their food-plants grow.

One such inhabitant of the wilderness, the swallowtail butterfly, is largely confined in Britain to open fenland in the Hickling/Horsey area of Broadland. Both the insect and its food-plant, milk parsley, occur at the Hickling Broad and Bure Marshes National Nature Reserves. Here the growth of bushes and trees is checked to retain the essential open character of the fen. Here, too, attempts are made to frustrate or control the activities of collectors who could easily reduce the swallowtail population to a level which would not allow this magnificent insect to recover from the harmful effects of gales, bad weather and other emergencies.

The first swallowtails emerge during May and the first half of June

Swallowtail butterfly

Swallowtail butterflies occur at two National Nature Reserves in Broadland.

when they may be seen basking in the sunshine, sipping nectar from flowers or patrolling the fen. The females lay their eggs on the milk parsley where larvae emerge and feed. At first resembling bird droppings, the larvae eventually become bright green with black, orange spotted markings. When alarmed, the larvae erect, as a form of protection, a pink forked contractile process which produces a strong scent resembling pineapples. They pass into the chrysalis stage in July or August after fixing themselves by silken threads to stems of sedges, reeds or bushes. Generally butterflies do not emerge from most of these chrysalids until the following year, but a few may appear and produce a second brood of larvae. These autumn larvae will feed not only on milk parsley but also on such other plants as angelica and ragged robin.

With a view to determining the best methods of managing the Broadland reserves for the swallowtail, scientists from Monks Wood Experimental Station are studying the population ecology of this rare insect on the Bure Marshes National Nature Reserve. Their work on other East Anglian reserves has demonstrated, for example, the serious effect of a series of bad summers on the small copper butterfly whose females will not lay their eggs unless the sun is shining. Disturbance of habitats, such as occurs when woods are cleared, can also have serious results. Many other factors affect the distribution and status of butterflies and other insects (and not only these creatures). Conservationists are often powerless, but on occasion they have been able to match concern with action.

Moths

This was the case when it became known that the only Suffolk habitat of the barberry carpet moth would be destroyed during the construction of the Bury St Edmunds by-pass. A piece of land was secured not far from the original site and here the Suffolk Trust for Nature Conservation planted 100 young plants of the common barberry, food-plant of this rare insect. Larvae and eggs of the barberry carpet moth were introduced there in the autumn of 1973, others being put on a large common barberry bush elsewhere. The outcome of the project is awaited with interest.

I referred in Chapter 2 (See p. 43) to the conservation in Breckland of the Spanish catchfly, food-plant of the viper's bugloss moth. Such work is considered vital in the case of rare plants, but it is no less important where common or widespread plants form the stronghold of isolated colonies of uncommon insects.

The common bindweed is, as its name suggests, abundant. But, as the food-plant of the spotted sulphur, it is of outstanding importance in Breckland where most British examples of this pretty black and yellow moth are found. In the same way, the flixweed, a widespread species, and the treacle mustard, a locally common weed, are eaten by the greenish larvae of the grey carpet, a greyish moth whose British habitats are restricted to Breckland. This last-named area is also noteworthy for the presence of the archer's dart, a moth chiefly found on sandy coasts, whose greenish grey larvae feed on several bedstraws and various common grasses.

Many of the moths breeding in Broadland are rare insects, but one of the most interesting is a common species, the peppered moth, whose larvae feed on rose and bramble and also on oak, birch and other trees. Its normal form, whose white wings 'peppered' with black afford the insect protection when resting on clean bark, occurs there, and so does the melanistic (black) form, which is conspicuous on clean bark but well camouflaged on sooty bark. Long regarded as the earliest example of industrial melanism, the dark variety of the peppered moth was first found in Manchester in 1848. In Broadland, where it has lived for at least fifty years, it is camouflaged against bark and foliage blackened by sooty moulds that develop on honeydew secreted by aphids.

The Broadland fauna also includes several moths which are unusual because of their aquatic larvae. Members of the family Pyraustidae, some of them enjoy the popular name of china-marks on account of their delicately patterned wings. The pale yellowish or greenish larvae of one species, the common *Nymphula stratiotata*, are completely aquatic, obtaining their oxygen from the water by means of thread-like gills. They spin silken webs among the leaves of water soldier or other water-plants, living and feeding there from summer until the following spring when they form submerged cocoons. The moths themselves are on the wing from June to September.

At one time the East Anglian fauna included several rare dragonflies, but in recent years the Nature Conservancy Council have appealed for information on the status of *Aeshna isosceles* and *Coenagrion armatum*, two species whose British stations were confined to Broadland. *Aeshna isosceles*, the Norfolk Aeshna, a magnificent early summer dragonfly, had its headquarters in the Ant valley. Here its favoured breeding sites were dykes and broads where the water soldier grew. It did not appear to have been recorded for several years, but in 1974 was positively identified in an area where it is thought to be fairly secure. First discovered at Sutton in 1903, *Coenagrion armatum* was mainly found in the vicinity of the river Ant. One worker spent a week searching for it at the best time of year in 1974 but without success. The loss of healthy aquatic conditions is considered to be the chief reason for the decline of dragonflies, and there is talk of replacing the lost habitat in the vital areas by clearing out dykes or by excavating new dykes or pools.

Dragonflies

Happily there are places in the region where dragonflies continue to thrive. Scarning Fen, a 10-acre reserve of the Norfolk Naturalists' Trust, is one such area. Here one may see the emperor dragonfly, our longest-bodied British insect, which attains 3 in. in length. Pashford Poors Fen, where members of the Suffolk Trust for Nature Conservation have been removing birch and willow and opening water holes, is a habitat of the southern Aeshna (*A. cyanea*). This dragonfly also occurs in Broadland, as does the large red damselfly (*Pyrrhosoma nymphula*), another Pashford species.

Bumblebees

As is supposed to be the case with dragonflies and their delicate relatives, the damselflies, it is commonly believed that the bumblebee population has declined in East Anglia in recent years. Although it is not always easy to establish beyond doubt the truth of such suggestions, it is certainly true that burning and tidying operations and the removal of hedgerows have helped to reduce the number of nest-sites for bumblebees, which have also suffered from the use of certain herbicides and insecticides. Despite such hazards, these important pollinators of red clover and lucerne (or alfalfa, as it is called in North America) are still seen in many parts of the region, including the towns.

Bombus pratorum, an early nesting species that forages on many different plants and nests in a great variety of places, is one of the most common bumblebees in East Anglia. Another is *Bombus agrorum*. Its nesting places are usually under tussocks of grass or moss on the surface of the ground, but one Norfolk queen of this species started her colony among the fruiting heads of freshly cut and stacked reeds. Both these bumblebees suffer from the attacks of cuckoo bumblebees of the genus *Psithyrus* whose six British species have been found in East Anglia. True to the name of cuckoo bumblebee, the parasitic *Psithyrus* female lays eggs in the nest of a bumblebee colony, leaving them to be reared by the *Bombus* workers.

Gall causers

Numerous other bees, wasps and related members of the Order Hymenoptera live in East Anglia where, as elsewhere, the galls caused by certain species attract far more attention than the insects themselves. Thus the bean-galls on willow and sallow leaves are much more conspicuous and familiar than the sawflies of the genus *Pontania* that cause them. The female of *Pontania proxima*, a very common species, lays its eggs in May in the leaf-buds and by June or July the pink or yellow-green coffee-bean shaped galls project from the leaf-blades. The larva eats out a cavity in the centre of the gall, eventually leaving through a hole on the lower side to pupate in the soil or on the bark of the tree. Many of the sawfly larvae are parasitised by ichneumons (these, too, are members of the Hymenoptera), and others may perish when a small black weevil lays its eggs in bean-galls.

Many gall-wasps – minute and insignificant relatives of bees – also cause conspicuous galls on oaks, wild roses and other plants (See p. 37) in East Anglia. They have been somewhat neglected here, but my own

Bumblebee. This forager is collecting pollen, an
essential food, from a bramble flower. The insect
packs pollen as it is collected into pollen-baskets
on its hind-legs. The pollen load is clearly seen in
this picture.

studies at Old Buckenham, and elsewhere in the region, show what a wealth of interest awaits naturalists who are prepared to study these insects. Considered in a wider context, these creatures are seen to play a part in nature which may well be more important than is generally realised. Certainly it is known that lesser spotted woodpeckers and other birds visit oak trees and attack the hard oak marble galls of the gall-wasp *Andricus kollari* to get at the larvae within. And pheasants take certain galls, as was evident when three ounces of oak spangle-galls, which are caused by gall-wasps (*Neuroterus* species) on oak leaves, were removed from the crop of one of these birds shot in November. Insect-eating birds must take a toll of the gall insects themselves.

Equally neglected by naturalists are the gall midges, minute flies, several of which are common and widespread in East Anglia. In Chapter 2 a few of the many wild plants that bear galls and other malformations caused by the larvae of gall midges are mentioned. Species such as the swede midge, the clover seed midge and the chrysanthemum midge attack cultivated crops and, because of the injury and loss they cause, have been classified as exceedingly harmful insects. On the other hand, certain gall midge larvae are enemies of troublesome aphids, each larva of one species having been found to consume 60 to 80 aphids during its 7-day growing period. Many other insects are attacked by gall midges and so are several species of mites, two of which are responsible for big bud galls on hazel and black currant respectively.

An example of the gall midges whose larvae feed on fungi was that obtained in Norfolk from a parasitic rust fungus on leaves of black currant. The leaves of this fruit crop are damaged by larvae of another gall midge, the black currant leaf midge, while its flowers are attacked by larvae of yet another gall midge, the black currant flower midge.

Gall midges do not seem to be of any real importance in the biological control of weeds, but some species become economically important when they transfer their attacks from wild plants to cultivated ones. The white larvae of one East Anglian species, the blackberry leaf midge, live in the leaves on growing shoots of wild brambles and cultivated blackberry and raspberry, causing distortion of leaves and, in severe infestations, stoppage of growth. Regular trimming of wild brambles in hedgerows has been recommended as one method of controlling this gall midge. The orange larvae of another East Anglian species, the blackberry or raspberry stem gall midge, cause walnut-shaped galls or irregular woody masses on stems of wild brambles and cultivated blackberry and raspberry. Plants bearing these galls produce few leaves and fruit, and affected raspberry canes are often attacked by a fungus. Control of this midge involves the collection and burning of all galls, including those from hedgerows. Gall midges have numerous natural enemies. Parasitic insects often attack the larvae, many of which are eaten by poultry and other birds, and late frosts may also kill them. It is likely, too, that certain gall midges and other gall-causing insects are affected by the cutting and spraying of roadside vegetation and by similar operations in other parts of the countryside.

I have yet to hear of deliberate attempts being made to conserve gall-causing insects in East Anglia. Scientists of Monks Wood Experimental Station have, however, studied the possible effects of cutting and spraying of hogweed on the life cycle of the minute fly *Phytomyza sphondylii*. The larvae of this leaf miner feed between the upper and lower epidermis of leaves of hogweed, a plant of road verges and meadows, making characteristic patterns or mines as they do so. Work on the insect fauna of the stinging nettle has called attention to several leaf mining flies occurring on this perennial herb.

Leaf miners

Unlike the species just mentioned, which appear to be confined to their single foodplants, some leaf-mining insects have many different plant hosts. The chrysanthemum leaf-miner, *Phytomyza atricornis*, a common East Anglian species, has over one hundred different ones. In the Earlham Park area of Norwich I found mines of this small fly on cultivated *Aster*, chrysanthemums, *Erigeron*, *Gaillardia*, lupins and garden peas and on such wild plants as burdock, mugwort, ragwort, groundsel, dandelion and sowthistle. Clearly if steps are ever taken to conserve leaf-mining insects they must, as should be the case with all insects, be based on a thorough knowledge of their habits, particularly their choice of foodplants.

Concern for the future of insect life cannot be confined to butterflies and moths or the larger and more colourful species if a rich and varied fauna is to be retained. This is becoming increasingly evident from the reports of workers in this field. For example, scientists of Monks Wood Experimental Station have recently emphasised that several rare and local beetles living at Staverton Park, Suffolk, must ultimately be at risk since there are no replacements for the ancient trees with which they are associated. Not being specialists, very few ordinary visitors notice beetles living in leaf litter in ancient hollow trees, in fungi and in rotten wood. But many other species commonly attract attention and they, too, are affected by such influences as changing land-use and weather conditions, the attacks of parasites and other enemies, and excessive tidying operations (many beetles live in and under dead birds and other animals, under rotten logs and dung).

Beetles

One beetle, the glow-worm, is killed in both the larval and adult stages in Broadland fens by the pale pink powdery fungus *Isaria fumoso-rosea*. In other parts of the region glow-worms are found on the top of sea-cliffs and on damp, grassy banks where they do not appear to be so

A living glow-worm
(top right) with the
remains of four others
killed by a fungus.

commonly attacked by this parasitic fungus. Although glow-worms may
be luminescent at all stages (even as eggs), most light is given out by the
earth-bound females, which use it as a 'sex-signal' to attract the males.
Adult glow-worms eat very little, if anything, but the larvae prey on
various species of snails and slugs. Thus there is no reason why active
steps should not be taken to conserve these beetles wherever they occur.

The same is true of the ladybirds or Coccinellidae and their larvae
whose destruction of aphids or plant-lice, carriers of the viruses of
diseases of the potato, sugar-beet and other plants, is of real economic
importance. There are beautiful yellow and yellow-and-black, spotted
and anchor-marked ladybirds, but the most familiar of the fifty or so
British species is the two-spot ladybird. Commonly this has red elytra
or wing-covers and two black spots, but it is variable in colour. The two-
spot is one of several ladybirds whose appearance in large numbers on
the East Anglian coast in summer gives rise on occasion to talk of plagues
and controversy as to whether the insects were invading migrants or
merely individuals bred at coastal habitats or those inland. Whatever
the truth may be in such cases, there is no doubt that East Anglia, with
its long coastline, is admirably placed to receive such migrants as red
admiral, painted lady and clouded yellow butterflies, and humming-
bird hawk, death's head and convolvulus hawk moths. Conservationists
cannot control their movements, but they can continue to provide and
maintain reserves where these migrants can, in company with resident
species, breed and thus increase the number and variety of East Anglian
insects.

List of East Anglian birds

Species are placed in alphabetical order for ease of reference.

Abbreviations: PM Passage migrant; RES Resident; SV Summer visitor; WV Winter visitor.

Auk, Little *Plautus alle* Irregular WV. Coastal waters, occasionally inland.

Avocet *Recurvirostra avosetta* PM, SV, occasional in winter. Breeds Havergate Island and Minsmere. Flooded marshes, estuaries, brackish pools.

Bee-eater *Merops apiaster* Very rare vagrant.

Bittern *Botaurus stellaris* RES, WV. Breeds Broadland and Minsmere. Reedbeds and swamps.

  Little *Ixobrychus minutus* Rare and irregular visitor. Probably bred in the past.

Blackbird *Turdus merula* RES, PM, WV. Common and widespread.

Blackcap *Sylvia atricapilla* Widespread and common SV, PM. A few winter here. Woodland, large gardens.

Bluethroat *Cyanosylvia svecica* Scarce passage visitor to coast, usually in autumn. Mainly red-spotted form, *C. s. svecica*. 'Singles' of white-spotted race, *C. s. cyanecula*, seen in April.

Brambling *Fringilla montifringilla* Irregular WV and PM. Some large flocks recorded. Beech, birch and conifer woods, stubble fields, mustard fields, coastal marshes.

Bullfinch *Pyrrhula pyrrhula* RES, common and widespread. Few examples of northern race, *P. p. pyrrhula*, recorded from Lowestoft-Yarmouth area, November/February.

Bunting, Cirl *Emberiza cirlus* Vagrant.

  Corn *E. calandra* A rather local resident. Cornfields, stubble fields, wasteland.

  Lapland *Calcarius lapponicus* PM, WV. Wasteland, saltings and marshes at coast. Usually small numbers, but flocks of 50–100 in N. Norfolk.

  Little *E. pusilla* Vagrant. Coast, September/February.

  Ortolan *E. hortulana* PM, autumn and spring. Coast, small numbers.

  Red-headed *E. bruniceps* Vagrant or 'escape' (large numbers are imported alive).

  Reed *E. schoeniclus* Abundant RES, PM, WV. Nests in reedbeds and marshes.

  Rustic *E. rustica* Vagrant. Coast.

  Snow *Plectrophenax nivalis* WV, mainly in coastal areas, rare inland.

Bustard, Great *Otis tarda* A former Breckland resident, but the native race long extinct in Britain. A few immigrant bustards have appeared this century.

Houbara *Chlamydotis undulata* Vagrant, 1962, making the fifth British record and the first this century.

  Little *O. tetrax* Scarce and irregular visitor. The eastern form, *O. t. orientalis*, from eastern Europe has occurred here.

Buzzard *Buteo buteo* Scarce visitor in spring, autumn and winter. Formerly bred. Seen coast and inland, mainly wooded areas.

  Honey *Pernis apivorus* Scarce passage visitor, mostly in autumn. Formerly bred.

  Rough-legged *B. lagopus* PM, WV, very scarce and irregular. Coastal marshes and heathland.

Chaffinch *Fringilla coelebs* Abundant and widespread RES, PM, WV.

Chiffchaff *Phylloscopus collybita* SV, PM. Very few have wintered here. Woodland, commons, large gardens.

Coot *Fulica atra* RES, breeding on lakes, Broads, meres, flooded gravel pits. Also WV.

Cormorant *Phalacrocorax carbo* PM, WV, non-breeding SV. Mainly coast, estuaries and Broads, but also inland. Formerly bred.

Corncrake *Crex crex* SV, PM, rare.

Courser, Cream-coloured *Cursorius cursor* Vagrant from N. Africa.

Crake, Baillon's *Porzana pusilla* Vagrant. Nested in Norfolk last century.

  Little *P. parva* Vagrant.

  Spotted *P. porzana* Mainly reported as scarce PM and WV, but has bred at Minsmere in recent years. Reedbeds, marshland.

Crane *Grus grus* Scarce visitor to coastal districts and Broads.

Crossbill *Loxia curvirostra* Local resident. Also irregular immigrant whose irruptions occur from late June onwards. Conifer trees and forests.

  Parrot *L. pytyopsittacus* Scarce vagrant.

  Two-barred *L. leucoptera* Scarce vagrant.

Crow, Carrion *Corvus corone corone* Common resident.

  Hooded *C. c. cornix* WV, PM, occasional SV. Mainly coastal districts.

Cuckoo *Cuculus canorus* Decreasing SV and PM.

  Great-spotted *Clamator glandarius* Vagrant.

  Yellow-billed *Coccyzus americanus* Gale-driven vagrant.

Curlew *Numenius arquata* SV, most nests in Breckland. WV, coast and estuaries. PM.

  Stone *Burhinus oedicnemus* SV, main stronghold in and around Breckland.

Dipper *Cinclus cinclus* Irregular WV to water-mills, weirs, old locks.

Diver, Black-throated *Gavia arctica* Uncommon WV, PM. Estuaries, Broads area.

Great northern *G. immer* Scarce WV, PM. Coast, tidal waters.

Red-throated *G. stellata* PM, WV. Parties in coastal waters, 'singles' visiting inland waters.

Dotterel *Eudromias morinellus* PM, usually very scarce. Coastal areas, fields inland.

Dove, Collared *Streptopelia decaocto* RES. Has spread over much of the country since it first bred in Britain at Cromer, Norfolk, in 1955.

Rock *Columba livia* Vagrant.

Rufous turtle *S. orientalis* Vagrant.

Stock *C. oenas* RES, PM, WV. Breeds in open woodland, parks, towers and ruins.

Turtle *S. turtur* SV, PM. Nests in tall hedges and thickets.

Dowitcher, Long-billed *Limnodromus scolopaceus* Vagrant.

Short-billed *L. griseus* Vagrant.

Duck, Ferruginous *Aythya nyroca* Scarce and irregular visitor.

Harlequin *Histrionicus histrionicus* Vagrant.

Long-tailed *Clangula hyemalis* WV, scarce. Occasional summer records (non-breeders). Mainly estuaries, harbours, coastal Broads. Few on inland waters.

Ring-necked *A. collaris* Vagrant.

Tufted *A. fuligula* Nests on suitable waters, mostly inland. Also WV and PM. Hard weather flocks on tidal waters.

Dunlin *Calidris alpina* PM, WV, some non-breeders in summer. Single pairs have bred, Norfolk. Coast and estuaries, inland beet factory settling ponds, sewage farms and lakes. Both southern (*C. a. schinzii*) and northern (*C. a. alpina*) races occur.

Dunnock *Prunella modularis* RES, common and widely distributed. PM.

Eagle, White-tailed *Haliaeëtus albicilla* Rare vagrant to coast, Hickling Broad and few inland lakes.

Egret, Cattle *Ardeola ibis* Vagrant.

Little *Egretta egretta* Vagrant to coastal areas.

Eider *Somateria mollissima* Non-breeders present all months. Coast, tidal waters, particularly north Norfolk coast.

Falcon, Gyr *Falco rusticolus* Vagrant. The one or two recent examples may have been 'escapes'.

Red-footed *F. vespertinus* Scarce and irregular visitor.

Fieldfare *Turdus pilaris* WV, PM. Variable numbers, but some large flocks.

Firecrest *Regulus ignicapillus* PM, scarce and irregular, coast. WV, few seen inland.

Flamingo *Phoenicopterus ruber* Occasional 'escapes' on coast.

Flycatcher, Collared *Muscicapa albicollis* Vagrant.

Pied *Ficedula hypoleuca* PM, most abundant in autumn. Coast and inland records.

Red-breasted *F. parva* PM, scarce, coast.

Spotted *M. striata* SV, widespread. PM. Parks, large gardens, woodland edge.

Fulmar *Fulmarus glacialis* SV, breeding on sea-cliffs in Norfolk. Also seen other months.

Gadwall *Anas strepera* RES, breeding in Broads district, Breckland, certain coastal areas, inland lakes.

Gannet *Sula bassana* Present off the coast all months. Occasional storm-driven birds inland.

Garganey *Anas querquedula* PM. SV, scarce, breeding regularly in Broads district, Ouse Washes, few coastal sites.

Godwit, Bar-tailed *Limosa lapponica* PM, WV, SV (non-breeders). Mudflats, saltings.

Black-tailed *L. limosa* PM. WV, coastal marshes and mudflats. SV, breeding on Ouse Washes and in Suffolk.

Goldcrest *Regulus regulus* RES, nesting in conifers, particularly in Breckland. Also PM, WV.

Goldeneye *Bucephala clangula* WV, PM. Coastal and inland waters. Large parties off Brancaster and at Hickling.

Goldfinch *Carduelis carduelis* RES, widespread and fairly common. PM. Some large winter flocks.

Goosander *Mergus merganser* WV, scarce, mainly to inland waters. Very few summer records.

Goose, Barnacle *Branta leucopsis* PM, WV, scarce and irregular. Breydon, N. Norfolk and Suffolk coasts.

Bean *Anser fabalis* WV, mostly to Yare Valley, Norfolk.

Brent *B. bernicla* PM. WV, mainly to wider Suffolk estuaries, Blakeney and Brancaster. Both dark-breasted (*B. b. bernicla*) and pale-breasted (*B. b. hrota*) races occur.

Canada *B. canadensis* Introduced RES, breeding on flooded gravel pits, lakes, rivers, broads, Breckland meres. Large numbers winter in north Norfolk at Holkham Park.

Egyptian *Alopochen aegyptiacus* Introduced RES whose largest full-winged colony is at Holkham Park.

Grey-lag *Anser anser* PM. WV, coastal grazing marshes, very scarce. Feral birds introduced and now well established in Broadland and elsewhere.

Lesser white-fronted *A. erythropus* Very scarce visitor, mainly to Lower Bure and Yare valleys.

Pink-footed *A. brachyrhynchus* PM, WV. Coast, Wash borders, Breydon.

Red-breasted *B. ruficollis* Vagrant.

Snow *A. caerulescens* Vagrant or 'escape'. North coast.

White-fronted *A. albifrons* WV, regularly to Breydon area, irregularly elsewhere on coast. The Greenland race (*A. a. flavirostris*) has been recorded.

Goshawk *Accipiter gentilis* A rare vagrant.

Grebe, Black-necked *Podiceps nigricollis* PM and WV, scarce. SV, irregular, non-breeding. Tidal waters, coastal broads.

Great-crested *P. cristatus* RES, breeding on broads, lakes, Breckland meres, flooded pits, moving to estuaries and coast for winter.

Little *P. ruficollis* RES. After breeding on lakes, broads, rivers, pits, ponds and dykes, moves to larger rivers and broads, coastal dykes and tidal waters.

Pied-billed *Podilymbus podiceps* Vagrant to Ouse Washes.

Red-necked *Podiceps griseigena* PM, WV, scarce. Coastal waters, larger broads.

Slavonian *P. auritus* PM, WV, scarce. Usually on coastal waters, but inland waters also visited.

Greenfinch *Chloris chloris* RES, WV, PM, widespread and common. Flocks seen autumn/winter.

Greenshank *Tringa nebularia* PM, casual WV. Coast, sewage farms, beet factory ponds, inland waters.

Grosbeak, Scarlet *Carpodacus erythrinus* Very rare vagrant.

Guillemot *Uria aalge* PM, WV to inshore waters. Both the southern (*U. a. albionis*) and northern (*U. a. aalge*) races recorded.

Black *Cepphus grylle* PM, WV, scarce. Coastal waters.

Gull, Black-headed *Larus ridibundus* SV, WV, PM, abundant. Breeding colonies on dunes, beaches and saltings, marshes, beet factory ponds, sewage farms.

Bonaparte's *L. philadelphia* Vagrant.

Common *L. canus* PM, WV, SV (non-breeding). Has nested at Blakeney Point, Minsmere and Scolt Head. Many flight inland to feed in winter.

Glaucous *L. hyperboreus* WV to parts of coast, small numbers.

Great black-backed *L. marinus* WV, PM, SV (non-breeding). Has nested on Suffolk coast.

In winter seen inland (feeds on town refuse dumps).

Great black-headed *L. ichthyaëtys* Vagrant.

Herring *L. argentatus* PM, WV, SV (usually non-breeding, but has bred). Seen inland at sewage farms and refuse dumps.

Iceland *L. glaucoides* WV, scarce. Coast.

Ivory *Pagophila eburnea* Recorded from Breydon Water.

Lesser black-backed *L. fuscus* PM, SV (usually non-breeding, but has bred), small numbers in winter. Coast, coastal broads and larger inland broads.

Little *L. minutus* PM, WV, SV (non-breeding). Coast, broads, Wisbech sewage farm, 'singles' or small parties. Exceptional inland.

Mediterranean black-headed *L. melanocephalus* Vagrant to coast.

Sabine's *Xema sabini* Vagrant to coast, rare and irregular.

Slender-billed *L. genei* 'Single', Minsmere, August.

Harrier, Hen *Circus cyaneus* WV, PM, usually 'singles'. Coastal areas, Breckland, Fenland Washes. Formerly bred.

Marsh *C. aeruginosus* WV, PM, SV, very scarce. Breeds Minsmere. Coast, broads, Fenland Washes.

Montagu's *C. pygargus* PM, very scarce. SV, few young raised. Coastal belt, Broadland, Breckland.

Hawfinch *Coccothraustes coccothraustes* RES, somewhat elusive. Mature deciduous woods and orchards.

Heron *Ardea cinerea* RES, WV, PM. Breeds at some 40 sites. River valleys, coastal marshes, tidal waters.

Night *Nycticorax nycticorax* A rare vagrant.

Purple *A. purpurea* A rare and irregular visitor. Broads, coastal belt.

Squacco *Ardeola ralloides* A rare vagrant. Broads.

Hobby *Falco subbuteo* Scarce PM. SV, has bred, but now thought to be non-breeding. Coastal area, Breckland.

Hoopoe *Upupa epops* PM, regular but scarce. Said to have bred in Suffolk last century.

Ibis, Glossy *Plegadis falcinellus* Rare vagrant.

Jackdaw *Corvus monedula* RES, abundant and widespread. PM, WV. The Scandinavian race, *C. m. monedula*, has been recorded.

Jay *Garrulus glandarius* RES, widespread and abundant in well-wooded areas. WV. The continental race, *G. g. glandarius*, has been recorded.

Kestrel *Falco tinnunculus* PM. RES, nesting sites include buildings and the ground (Broadland).

Kingfisher *Alcedo atthis* RES, widespread. Inland waters. Also seen on coast and Broads, autumn/winter.

Kite *Milvus milvus* Scarce and irregular visitor. Formerly bred.

 Black *M. migrans* A vagrant. Coast, May/June.

Kittiwake *Rissa tridactyla* WV, PM, SV. Breeds at Lowestoft. Coast, harbours. Occasional 'singles' inland.

Knot *Calidris canutus* PM, WV, SV (non-breeding). Tidal mudflats, exceptional inland. Large summer and winter flocks recorded in the Wash.

Lapwing *Vanellus vanellus* PM, WV, RES. Still widespread but no longer nesting very widely.

Lark, Short-toed *Calandrella brachydactyla* A rare vagrant. Coast.

Linnet *Carduelis cannabina* PM, WV, RES, widespread. Heaths, commons, hedges.

Magpie *Pica pica* RES, widespread, but a marked decline in many places.

Mallard *Anas platyrhynchos* WV, PM, RES. Widespread on waters and marshes, coast and inland.

Martin, House *Delichon urbica* Widespread and locally plentiful SV, PM.

 Sand *Riparia riparia* Local SV, abundant PM.

Merganser, Red-breasted *Mergus serrator* WV, PM. Occasional in summer. Mainly coastal waters, but 'singles' inland on broads, lakes, rivers.

Merlin *Falco columbarius* WV, PM. Coast, mostly 'singles'.

Moorhen *Gallinula chloropus* RES, common and widespread. WV, PM.

Nightingale *Luscinia megarhyncha* Local SV, PM. Thickets in woods and on heaths and commons.

Nightjar *Caprimulgus europaeus* SV, local, decreasing. Heaths, commons, wasteland. PM, scarce at coast.

Nutcracker, Slender-billed *Nucifraga caryocatactes macrorhynchos* A vagrant from N. Europe whose irruptions are irregular. Mainly August/October.

Nuthatch *Sitta europaea* RES, widespread, fairly common. Old deciduous woods, parks.

Oriole, Golden *Oriolus oriolus* SV, PM, spring, occasional in autumn. Very scarce, coast and inland. Young found, Breck borders, Norfolk, 1972. Bred Suffolk, 1973.

Osprey *Pandion haliaetus* PM, scarce, coastal and inland waters.

Ouzel, Ring *Turdus torquatus* PM, small numbers. Coast, also inland, 'singles' or small parties.

Owl, Barn *Tyto alba* The white-breasted race (*T. a. alba*) is a somewhat local resident, while the dark-breasted race (*T. a. guttata*) is a vagrant from N. Europe.

Little *Athene noctua* RES, widespread but decreased.

Long-eared *Asio otus* RES, local. PM, WV. Coniferous woods, old hawthorns. Broads, coast, Breckland.

Scops *Otus scops* Vagrant.

Short-eared *Asio flammeus* Scarce breeding bird. PM, WV, variable numbers. On and near coast, Broadland, Breckland.

Snowy *Nyctea scandiaca* Vagrant.

Tawny *Strix aluco* RES, widespread. Well-wooded areas, also towns.

Tengmalm's *Aegolius funereus* Vagrant.

Oystercatcher *Haematopus ostralogus* SV, breeding mainly at coast, particularly in N. Norfolk. PM, WV. Large autumn/winter flocks in The Wash and on N. Norfolk coast.

Partridge *Perdix perdix* RES, widespread but has declined.

Red-legged *Alectoris rufa* RES, widespread, reduced in many areas but still seen in places where common partridge has disappeared.

Peregrine *Falco peregrinus* WV, PM, scarce. Coast, Breckland. Formerly bred.

Petrel, Leach's *Oceanodroma leucorhoa* Rare and irregular visitor. Coastal waters. Storm-driven individuals occasionally inland.

Storm *Hydrobates pelagicus* Scarce autumn visitor. Coastal waters.

Phalarope, Grey *Phalaropus fulicarius* Autumn PM, WV, scarce. Coastal waters, inland ponds and pools.

Red-necked *P. lobatus* PM, scarce. Tidal waters, coastal and Broadland pools and dykes.

Wilson's *P. tricolor* Scarce visitor, Minsmere, Wisbech Sewage Farm, Hickling. June/November.

Pheasant *Phasianus colchicus* RES, widespread, artificially reared on sporting estates.

Golden *Chrysolophus pictus* Introduced breeder, well established in Breckland localities.

Pintail *Anas acuta* PM, WV, irregular SV. Has bred. Coast, Ouse Washes and other flooded levels, certain inland waters.

Pipit, Meadow *Anthus pratensis* RES. WV, PM, abundant. Coast and inland.

Red-throated *A. cervinus* Vagrant at N. Norfolk coast, May/June.

Richard's *A. richardi* Scarce and irregular visitor, spring, autumn. Coast.

Rock *A. spinoletta petrosus* WV, abundant,

coast. Scandinavian race (*A. s. littoralis*) is PM, coast, spring. Water pipit (*A. s. spinoletta*) is PM, WV, very scarce, coast, Hickling.

Tawny *A. campestris* Vagrant. Coast, 'singles', May/June, August/October.

Tree *A. trivialis* PM. SV, scarce. local. Heaths, commons, young conifer plantations.

Water See under Pipit, Rock.

Plover, Golden *Pluvialis apricaria* PM, WV, widespread but local. Marshes, fields, airfields. The northern race, *P. a. altifrons*, is a spring PM.

Grey *P. squatarola* PM, WV, SV (non-breeding). Mainly tidal mudflats, but some inland.

Kentish *Charadrius alexandrinus* Scarce PM. Has nested. Breydon, coast, Wisbech Sewage Farm.

Little ringed *C. dubius* PM, SV, scarce. Breeds mainly at working sand and gravel pits.

Ringed *C. hiaticula* SV, PM, WV. Shingle beaches, Breckland fields and heaths. The Arctic race, *C. h. tundrae*, is recorded as PM.

Sociable *Chettusia gregaria* Scarce visitor. Havergate.

Pochard *Aythya ferina* WV, PM, SV. Nests on inland waters, including sites in Breckland and Broadland.

Red-crested *Netta rufina* A rare visitor. Coast, Broadland.

White-eyed See under Duck, Ferruginous.

Pratincole, Black-winged *Glareola nordmanii* Vagrant. Cley.

Puffin *Fratercula arctica* Scarce PM, WV. Coastal waters.

Quail *Coturnix coturnix* Very scarce SV, breeding on farmland where heard calling.

Rail, Water *Rallus aquaticus* RES, WV, PM, secretive. Reedbeds, swamps, dykes.

Raven *Corvus corax* Rare vagrant. Formerly bred.

Razorbill *Alca torda* PM, WV. Coastal waters.

Redpoll, Arctic *Carduelis hornemanni* Scarce visitor, mainly coast, September/January. Both *C. h. hornemanni* and Coues's race, *C. h. exilipes*, recorded.

Greenland *C. flammea rostrata* 'Single' recorded, December.

Lesser *C. flammea cabaret* Breeds in young conifer plantations, and birch scrub. Somewhat local but not uncommon.

Mealy *C. flammea flammea* Scarce WV.

Redshank *Tringa totanus* RES, PM. Breeds saltings, coastal grazing marshes, river valleys. Continental, *T. t. totanus*, and Icelandic, *T. t. robusta*, forms are PM, WV.

Spotted *T. erythropus* PM, WV, some oversummer. Coast, Hickling, Sewage farms,

Breckland meres. Usually 'singles' or small parties.

Redstart *Phoenicurus phoenicurus* PM, SV, local. Breeds woodland, particularly Breckland oakwoods.

Black *P. obscurus* SV, local, has nested in several towns. Also PM, WV.

Redwing *Turdus iliacus* WV, PM, usually abundant, regular. Marshes, farmland. Visits towns and gardens in hard weather.

Robin *Erithacus rubecula* RES, common, widespread. The Continental race, *E. r. rubecula*, is PM, WV.

Roller *Coracias graculus* A rare vagrant.

Rook *Corvus frugilegus* RES, abundant, widespread. PM, WV.

Ruff *Philomachus pugnax* After long absence as breeding species, nests found on Norfolk stretch of Ouse Washes, 1970. PM, WV. Coast, Broads, Sewage Farms, Beet Factory ponds.

Sanderling *Crocethia alba* PM, WV, SV (non-breeding). Sandy beaches, The Wash (large autumn gatherings), mudflats.

Sand-grouse, Pallas's *Syrrhaptes paradoxus* A very rare vagrant.

Sandpiper, Baird's *Calidris bairdii* A vagrant. Coast, Wisbech Sewage Farm, August/October.

Bartram's *Bartramia longicauda* 'Single', Minsmere, 1964.

Broad-billed *Limicola falcinellus* Rare vagrant. Coast, Wisbech Sewage Farm, May/June, August/September.

Buff-breasted *Tryngites subruficollis* A very rare vagrant. 'Singles', coast, May, September/October.

Common *Tringa hypoleucos* PM, occasional SV (has nested), occasionally winters here. Coast and inland waters.

Curlew *Calidris testacea* PM, irregular. Coast, beet factory settling ponds, Sewage farms.

Green *Tringa ochropus* WV, PM. Fresh-water, beet factory settling ponds, Sewage farms.

Marsh *T. stagnatilis* Very scarce visitor. Coast.

Pectoral *Calidris melanotos* Scarce visitor. Coast, Wisbech Sewage Farm, Autumn.

Purple *C. maritima* PM, WV, scarce. Coast, shingle.

Semi-palmated *C. pusilla* Vagrant. Cley, Minsmere, Wisbech Sewage Farm. July, September, November/December.

Solitary *Tringa solitaria* Vagrant. Hickling, coast. August/September.

Spotted *T. macularia* Vagrant. Cley.

Stilt *Micropalma himantopus* Vagrant. Wisbech Sewage Farm, Minsmere. July/August.

Terek *Tringa terek* Southwold, June 1951.

Upland See under Sandpiper, Bartram's.

White-rumped *Calidris fuscicollis* Vagrant. Minsmere, Wisbech Sewage Farm, July/November.

Wood *Tringa glareola* PM, irregular. SV, occasional, non-breeding. Coast, freshwater.

Scaup *Aythya marila* WV, PM, very variable numbers. A few over-summer. The Wash, other tidal waters. Inland waters in hard weather.

Scoter, Common *Melanitta nigra* WV, PM, non-breeders in summer. Mainly on coastal waters, few on Broads and Breckland meres.

Surf *M. perspicillata* Vagrant. Coast, October/November.

Velvet *M. fusca* WV, PM. Inshore waters.

Serin *Serinus canarius* Vagrant, mainly coast.

Shag *Phalacrocorax aristotelis* Autumn and winter visitor, scarce, irregular. Tidal waters.

Shearwater, Cory's *Puffinus diomedea borealis* Vagrant. Coast.

Great *P. gravis* Vagrant. Coastal waters. August/January.

Little *P. baroli baroli* Vagrant. April/May.

Manx *P. puffinus* PM, autumn. Coastal waters, mainly N. Norfolk. Balearic race, *P. p. mauretanicus*, recorded, N. Norfolk, autumn.

Sooty *P. grisea* Autumn visitor, irregular. Coastal waters.

Shelduck *Tadorna tadorna* SV, PM, WV. Mainly coast, but some breed inland.

Ruddy *T. ferruginea* Rare vagrant. Some occurrences may be 'escapes'.

Shorelark *Eremophila alpestris* WV, somewhat scarce. Coast.

Shoveler *Anas clypeata* PM, WV, SV. Nests Broadland, coastal marshes, Breckland.

Shrike, Great grey *Lanius excubitor* WV, PM. Heaths, tall hawthorn hedges. Coast and inland.

Lesser grey *L. minor* Vagrant. Coast, May/June, September/October.

Red-backed *L. cristatus* SV, PM, scarce. Heaths, tall hedges. Coastal belt, Breckland.

Woodchat *L. senator* Scarce visitor, mainly spring.

Siskin *Carduelis spinus* PM, WV. Attracted to alders and birches. Large 'irruptions' noted in certain years.

Skua, Arctic *Stercorarius parasiticus* PM, mainly in autumn. Coastal waters.

Great *S. skua* PM, scarce. Coastal waters.

Long-tailed *S. longicauda* PM, autumn, scarce. Inshore waters.

Pomarine *S. pomarinus* PM, mainly autumn, small numbers. Inshore waters.

Skylark *Alauda arvensis* RES, PM, WV. Widespread, abundant.

Smew *Mergus albellus* WV. Coastal broads, estuaries, inland waters. More abundant in hard winters.

Snipe *Gallinago gallinago* RES, PM, WV. Nests in boggy places, marshes, commons, but a diminishing breeding species.

Great *G. media* Scarce visitor.

Jack *Lymnocryptes minimus* WV, PM. Bogs, marshes, saltings.

Sparrow, Hedge See under Dunnock.

House *Passer domesticus* RES, common, widespread. PM.

Tree *P. montanus* RES, common, widespread. PM, WV.

White-throated *Zonotrichia albicollis* Vagrant. Lowestoft, November 1968 – January 1969.

Sparrowhawk *Accipiter nisus* RES, very scarce. PM, WV. Well-wooded areas, coast, Breckland.

Spoonbill *Platalea leucorodia* PM, SV (non-breeding). Formerly bred. Coast, Hickling, Breydon.

Starling *Sturnus vulgaris* RES, PM, WV. Abundant. Large autumn/winter communal roosts in reedbeds, trees and shrubs.

Rosy *S. roseus* A vagrant.

Stilt, Black-winged *Himantopus himantopus* A rare vagrant. Coastal areas.

Stint, Little *Calidris minuta* PM. Mainly coastal areas, Wisbech Sewage Farm. Some larger gatherings in autumn.

Temminck's *C. temminckii* PM, scarce. Coast, Wisbech Sewage Farm. 'Singles' or very small parties.

Stonechat *Saxicola torquata* Now a scarce breeding bird. Also PM, WV (mainly coast). Furze heaths, commons, dunes.

Stork, Black *Ciconia nigra* A very rare vagrant. Coast.

White *C. ciconia* A rare vagrant. Coast.

Swallow *Hirundo rustica* SV, PM, common, widespread.

Red-rumped *H. daurica* Vagrant. Blakeney, Mundesley, 'singles', March/April.

Swan, Bewick's *Cygnus columbianus* PM, WV. Coastal and inland waters.

Mute *C. olor* RES, breeding on inland waters and saltings of tidal rivers. Some large winter concentrations, estuaries, Ipswich docks, Hickling.

Whooper *C. cygnus* PM, WV. Coastal and inland waters, including Ouse Washes and Breckland meres.

Swift *Apus apus* SV, PM, fairly abundant. Breeds in towns and villages.

Alpine *A. melba* A rare vagrant, May/September.

Teal *Anas crecca crecca* RES, WV, PM. Breeds coastal belt, river valleys, Breckland, Ranworth area. More widely distributed autumn/winter.

Blue-winged *A. discors* A rare vagrant. 'Singles', Hardley Flood, R. Deben and Minsmere. April, October, December.

Green-winged *A. crecca carolinensis* Vagrant. Cley, April.

Tern, Arctic *Sterna paradisea* PM, also SV, a few pairs breeding N. Norfolk coast, Havergate Island.

Black *Chlidonias niger* PM, SV (non-breeding, occasional). Formerly bred in Broadland and the Fens. 2 pairs bred, Ouse Washes, Norfolk/Cambridgeshire, 1966. Seen estuaries, inland waters, coast.

Caspian *Sterna caspia* A vagrant. Coast, Hickling. June/July, September/October.

Common *S. hirundo* PM, SV. Breeds Broadland and on coast (N. Norfolk, Minsmere, Havergate). Also seen inland waters, including Breckland meres.

Gull-billed *Gelochelidon nilotica* Scarce visitor. Coast, Hickling, Breydon. May/June, August.

Little *Sterna albifrons* PM, SV, main breeding on coast, N. Norfolk (particularly Blakeney Point), E. Norfolk, Orfordness, Minsmere.

Roseate *S. dougallii* SV, PM, rare. N. Norfolk coast, Havergate, Minsmere. Has bred, N. Norfolk.

Sandwich *S. sandvicensis* SV, PM. Breeds on coast, N. Norfolk (large colony at Scolt Head), Minsmere.

Sooty *S. fuscata* A very rare vagrant. 'Singles' N. Norfolk coast, Breckland, April, June/July, September.

Whiskered *Chlidonias hybrida* A rare vagrant. 'Singles' Hickling, coast. May/July, October.

White-winged black *C. leucopterus* Scarce visitor, mainly spring. Usually 'singles' but some small parties. Coast, Breydon, Hickling, Wisbech Sewage Farm.

Thrush, Mistle *Turdus viscivorus* RES, widespread, fairly abundant. Well-wooded areas. Also PM, WV.

Rock *Monticola saxatilis* 'Single', Salthouse, 1969.

Song *T. philomelos* RES, common, widespread. Partial migrant, PM, WV.

Tit, Bearded *Panurus biarmicus* Resident breeder, local irruptive visitor. Reedbeds. Broadland, N. Norfolk coastal marshes, Minsmere.

Blue *Parus caeruleus* RES, widespread, abundant. WV. Examples of continental race, *P. c. caeruleus,* identified at coast.

Coal *P. ater* RES. Mainly conifer woods of Breckland, coastal belt. Continental race, *P. a. ater,* identified on autumn passage.

Great *P. major* RES, common, widespread. Continental race, *P. m. major,* is PM, WV.

Long-tailed *Aegithalos caudatus* RES, deciduous woods, hedges, thickets, uncultivated areas. Northern race, *A. c. caudatus,* recorded at N. Norfolk coast.

Marsh *P. palustris* RES, widespread but rather local. Deciduous woods.

Willow *P. montanus* RES, widespread but local. Breckland, Broadland, coastal belt and elsewhere.

Treecreeper *Certhia familiaris* RES, widespread. Woods. Northern form, *C. f. familiaris,* recorded.

Turnstone *Arenaria interpres* PM, WV, SV (non-breeding). Coastal mudflats, salt marshes, Wisbech Sewage Farm, Hickling.

Twite *Carduelis flavirostris* WV, PM. Coast, salt marshes, Wisbech Sewage Farm, Ouse Washes, occasionally Breckland.

Wagtail, Ashy-headed *Motacilla flava cinereocapilla* Scarce visitor, Cley, April/May.

Black-headed *M. flava feldegg* Scarce visitor, Cley, April, June.

Blue-headed *M. flava flava* Scarce PM. Single pairs have bred.

Grey *M. cinerea* SV, scarce. PM, WV. Water-mills, rivers, streams, ponds, sewage farms.

Grey-headed *M. flava thunbergi* Rare passage visitor. Coast, Hickling. May, September.

Pied *M. alba yarrellii* RES, widespread, abundant. WV, PM.

Sykes's *M. flava beema* Birds identical with this race have bred, but may have been hybrids.

White *M. alba alba* PM, scarce.

Yellow *M. flava flavissima* SV, PM. Heaths, marshes. Breckland, coastal belt.

Yellow-headed *M. citreola* Scarce visitor, autumn.

Warbler, Aquatic *Acrocephalus paludicola* Scarce visitor, autumn. Mainly N. Norfolk coast.

Arctic *Phylloscopus borealis* Vagrant. 'Singles', N. Norfolk coast, September/October.

Barred *Sylvia nisoria* PM, mainly autumn, scarce. Coast, particularly N. Norfolk.

Bonelli's *P. bonelli* Scarce visitor. Coast, N. Norfolk, Minsmere. April/May, August.

Cetti's *Cettia cetti* Scarce visitor. Minsmere, Norwich, March/June.

Dusky *P. fuscatus* Scarce visitor. Coast, N. Norfolk, October/November.

Garden *S. borin* SV, local, open woodland with undergrowth. Also PM, coast, mainly autumn.

Grasshopper *Locustella naevia* SV, local, Broadland, river valleys, dry woods and commons with brambles. Also PM.

Great reed *A. arundinaceus* Vagrant, 'singles', Minsmere, Horning, June/August.

Greenish *P. trochiloides* Scarce visitor, coast, N. Norfolk, August/November.

Icterine *Hippolais icterina* PM, very rare, mainly autumn. Coast, Minsmere, N. Norfolk.

Melodious *H. polyglotta* Scarce visitor. Coast, Cley, Minsmere, June/September.

Pallas's leaf *P. proregulus* Scarce visitor. Coast, N. Norfolk, Minsmere, also Norwich. October/November.

Radde's bush *P. schwarzi* Scarce visitor. Coast, N. Norfolk, Minsmere. October.

Reed *A. scirpaceus* SV, widespread, reedbeds. PM.

Sardinian *S. melanocephala* Vagrant. One at Waxham, Norfolk, April, 1973.

Savi's *L. luscinioides* SV, breeding in reedbeds, Minsmere, Walberswick. Also recorded Cley, Wisbech Sewage Farm.

Sedge *A. schoenobaenus* SV, PM, abundant, widespread. Usually nests in damp places, but has also bred in fields and other dry situations.

Subalpine *S. cantillans* Vagrant. Blakeney, Cley, May/June, September.

Willow *P. trochilus* PM, SV, abundant, woods, heaths. Northern race, *P. t. acredula*, is scarce PM.

Wood *P. sibilatrix* SV, PM, local, very scarce.

Yellow-browed *P. inornatus* Scarce visitor, coast, mainly N. Norfolk, Minsmere, autumn. 'Single' wintered Cley.

Waxwing *Bombycilla garrulus* WV, irregular irruptions. Attracted to berried trees and shrubs, even in towns.

Wheatear *Oenanthe oenanthe* SV, local, Breckland, coastal heaths and warrens. PM, including Greenland race, *O. o. leucorrhoa*.

Black-eared *O. hispanica* Vagrant. Salthouse, August/September 1965.

Desert *O. deserti* Vagrant. Blakeney.

Whimbrel *Numenius phaeopus* PM, occasional SV (non-breeding). Coast and vicinity.

Whinchat *Saxicola rubetra* PM, chiefly autumn. SV, very local, Breckland, Ouse Washes, Minsmere, wasteland. Numbers low.

Whitethroat *Sylvia communis* SV, PM, abundant, widespread.

Lesser *S. curruca* SV, local. PM.

Wigeon *Anas penelope* PM, WV. Coastal waters, inland lakes, rivers, larger Broads, Breckland meres. Has bred Hickling and N. Norfolk coast. Large numbers in severe weather.

American *A. americana* Cley, 1967, 1969, November.

Woodcock *Scolopax rusticola* RES, WV, PM. Breeds in woodlands, forestry plantations. Increasing.

Woodlark *Lullula arborea* RES, very local, mainly Breckland, Suffolk coastal belt.

Woodpecker, Great spotted *Dendrocopus major* RES, widespread, fairly common, old woodlands (*D. m. anglicus*). Northern race, *D. m. major*, is PM, WV.

Green *Picus viridis* RES, widespread, not uncommon. Coastal belt, Breckland, wooded country.

Lesser spotted *D. minor* RES, local. Old deciduous woods, open-timbered parkland.

Woodpigeon *Columba palumbus* RES, WV, abundant, widespread. Woods, farmland.

Wren *Troglodytes troglodytes* RES, widespread, common. PM, autumn.

Wryneck *Jynx torquilla* SV, PM, scarce.

Yellowhammer *Emberiza citrinella* RES, WV, PM, common. Hedges, commons.

Yellowlegs, Lesser *Tringa flavipes* Vagrant. Wisbech Sewage Farm, Minsmere, Havergate Island. August/September.

Nature reserves and other places to visit

East Anglia abounds in places suitable for nature rambles and picnics, but it is hoped that the following alphabetical list of nature reserves, country and wildlife parks, walks and picnic places will assist not only visitors to the region but residents venturing into less familiar areas.

The numbers used in the list also appear on the map of East Anglia on pages 8 and 9. Thus by using the list of places to visit in conjunction with the map the reader can plan suitable outings.

The following abbreviations are used:

LNR	Local Nature Reserve
m	mile(s)
NCCEA	Nature Conservancy Council East Anglia Region
NNR	National Nature Reserve
NNT	Norfolk Naturalists' Trust
NR	Nature Reserve
NT	National Trust
NWR	National Wildfowl Refuge
PAR	Permit required to visit parts away from the rights of way
PS	Picnic site
PVR	Permit to visit required
RSPB	Royal Society for the protection of Birds
RWR	Regional Wildfowl Refuge
SPNR	Society for the Promotion of Nature Reserves
SSSI	Site of Special Scientific Interest
STNC	Suffolk Trust for Nature Conservation

The map references in the list enable places to be located on maps of the Ordnance Survey, the AA *Road Book*, and others bearing the National Grid.

Readers are reminded that no attempt should be made to collect specimens or to carry out research unless written permission has previously been obtained. Where necessary, applications for permits should be made *well in advance* of the dates of proposed visits. Always keep letters brief and to the point and enclose a fully stamped and addressed envelope if a reply is requested.

Every effort has been made to ensure that details are correct at the time of going to press, but visitors should check those which might change before setting out.

Aldewood Forest 1
Suffolk. Picnic places: TM 355500 on B 1084, 6m E of Woodbridge; TM465710 off B 1125, 3m SSE of Blythburgh in SE direction towards Dunwich; TM 465010, 1m N of Fritton village.

Banham Zoo 2
TM 0687. Norfolk: 7m NW of Diss on B 1113. Animals and birds from all parts of the world. Open daily. Admission fee. Free car park. Picnic areas.

Barton Broad 3
TG 3621. Broadland: Ant valley. NR, SSSI. 355 acres. Open water surrounded by fen and carr. Broad open to pleasure boats.

Beeston Regis Heath 4
TG 173418. Norfolk coast, adjoining West Runton 'Roman Camp'. NT Open Space. 37 acres. Open and wooded heathland. Free access at all times. Footpath access from Brittons and Calves Well Lanes. Car parking at West Runton 'Roman Camp' only.

Blakeney Point 5
TG 0046. North Norfolk coast. NR, NT, SSSI. 1,335 acres. Shingle, sand dunes, salt marshes. Access to ternery restricted May – July. Access on foot: walk W from Cley along shingle bank. By boat: from Morston and Blakeney about 2 hours before or after high tide (Consult local boatmen).

Blickling Hall 6
TG 1729 – 1728. Norfolk: 1m NW of Aylsham (A 140). NT. Hall and gardens, park, woods and lake. Access seasonal, admission fee. Picnicking allowed in parts of the park and certain roadside woodland areas.

Bradfield Woods 7
TL 930573. Suffolk: 6m SE of Bury St Edmunds. NR, SPNR. Public normally admitted to the rides only. Naturalists interested in research should consult Secretary of Management Committee, Lavender Cottage, Great Waldingfield, Sudbury, Suffolk C010 0TN. 100 acres. Woodland managed both for its wildlife and its coppice produce. *Notes for visitors* and other priced publications available from Secretary (See above).

Brancaster Manor 8
TF 800450. North Norfolk coast. NT. Foreshore, sand dunes, reclaimed marshland, salt marshes. Car park at N end of road to beach from Brancaster village (approach road liable to flooding at high spring tides).

Brandon Park 9
TL 7885. Breckland: 1m S of Brandon on B 1106. Country Park, approved by Countryside Com-

mission, managed by Suffolk County Council. 31 acres. Free access.

Breydon Water 10
TG 4706 – 5108. Norfolk-Suffolk: immediately inland from Great Yarmouth. LNR. 2,000 acres. Estuary, about 3m by 1m. 3 mile walk along S shore: from Burgh Castle (turn right past church) or from railway bridge (pass underneath) at Great Yarmouth.

Bure Marshes 11
TG 3216 – 3515. Broadland: Bure valley, 9m NE of Norwich. NNR. 1019 acres (200 woodland). Aquatic, fen and marsh communities. Includes Hoveton Great, Ranworth, Decoy and Cockshoot Broads. Nature Trail at Hoveton Great Broad open daily (except Saturdays), first Monday in May until mid-Sept. Can only be reached by boat. Parts away from Nature Trail: PVR, refer NCCEA. Leaflet from NCCEA. Booklet from Trail Warden.

Cavenham Heath 12
TL 7672. Breckland: 1m W of Icklingham. NNR. 376 acres. Typical Breck heathland, low-lying areas of wet heath, fen carr. PVR, refer NCCEA, for Ash Plantation, Cavenham Poors' Heath and Tuddenham Poors' Heath. Access to rest of reserve unrestricted. Small car park and picnic site at Temple Bridge.

Clare Castle and Bailey 13
TL 7745. Suffolk: between Clare village and River Stour. Country Park, approved by the Countryside Commission, managed by Suffolk County Council. 23 acres. River and moat, woodland, scrub and thicket, open grassed areas. Free access.

Cley Marshes (including Arnold's marsh) 14
TG 0544. North Norfolk coast: Warden's House and Observation Hut are on S side of A 149 about ½m E of Cley village. Statutory Bird Sanctuary, SSSI. Cley marshes: 435 acres. Arnold's Marsh: 29 acres. Coastal marshes. Access to East Bank unrestricted. Otherwise bird watching facilities open to limited number of permit holders daily from 1 April to 31 October (except Mondays). Applications for day permits, including use of Observation Hut and hides, to NNT at Norwich at least one week in advance (fee payable). Unsold permits of a day's quota available from Cley Warden after 10a.m. 1 November to 31 March: restricted facilities by advance application. Car park on coast road. Pamphlets *History of Cley Marshes* and *Cley Marshes Nature Reserve* sold by NNT. Also see *Check-list of the birds of Cley and neighbouring parishes* (R. A. Richardson, 1962).

Dersingham 15
Norfolk. TF 683294. Picnic site by A 149.

Dunwich Heath 16
TM 475683. Suffolk coast: between Southwold and Aldeburgh, turn right off the Westleton-Dunwich road ½m before reaching Dunwich. NT Open Space. 214 acres. Heathland with sandy cliffs and over a mile of beach and foreshore. Fine view S over adjoining Minsmere bird reserve (RSPB). Access at all times. Car park (small charge). NT priced brochure available.

Easton Farm Park 17
Suffolk: 6m N of Woodbridge. Country Park, approved by the Countryside Commission, managed by J. M. Kerr. 32½ acres.

East Wretham Heath 18
TL 9188. Breckland: 4m N of Thetford. NR, SSSI. 362 acres. Heath, woodland, meres (Langmere, Ringmere). Access at Warden's Office, NE corner of reserve on A 1075. Nature Trail: open daily (except Tuesdays), 1 April – 30 Sept. to limited number of visitors. Permit and brochure (fee payable) from Warden. Hide overlooking Langmere: day permits (except Tuesdays) from Warden (fee payable). Brochure sold by NNT.

Felbrigg Woodland Walk 19
TQ 394193. Norfolk coast: 2m SW of Cromer, off A 148. NT. 1 mile walk. Old parkland, small area of heathland, fine old trees. Walk starts and ends at gate from main gardens behind Orangery at Felbrigg Hall. Open daily (except Fridays, Saturdays and Mondays other than Bank Holiday Monday), 2–6p.m., April – mid-Oct. Entrance charge except to NT members. NT sells brochure with map.

Flatford Mill and Judas Gap Marsh 20
TM 077332. Suffolk: on N bank of River Stour, 1m S of East Bergholt (B 1070). NT. Let to Field Studies Council as Field Centre for teaching and research. Mill not open to the public. JUDAS GAP MARSH 5½ acres. Access by application to Field Studies Council.

Fritton Lake 21
TG 4800. A Broadland water between Great Yarmouth and Lowestoft, off A 143. Covers 170 acres, follows a winding course of nearly 3 miles, and is surrounded by wooded shores. Picnic area, coarse fishing, boating. Open Easter – September. Admission fee.

Groton Wood 22
TL 977432. Suffolk: 2m NE of Boxford, 2m SW of Kersey. NR, STNC. 50 acres. Ancient small-leaved lime coppice, secondary woodlands (standard trees and small coppice), earthworks and ponds. Access through gates into rides in SW and

SE corners. Open to STNC members at any time. Others should seek permission from STNC Secretary.

Haughley 23

Suffolk: 2½m W of Stowmarket on A 45. Picnic site approved by the Countryside Commission, managed by Suffolk County Council. 9½ acres. Free access.

Havergate Island 24

TM 425496. Suffolk coast: near Orford. RSPB Reserve, part of Orfordness-Havergate NNR and NWR. 265 acres. Island with saltings and lagoons. PVR, Apply Havergate Warden, Orford, Woodbridge, Suffolk 1P12 2LX (but first obtain details of visiting arrangements and permit charges from January-February issue of *Birds* or RSPB). Access by boat from Orford quay (permit holders only). Binoculars can be hired.

Hickling Broad 25

TG 4122. Broadland: Thurne valley. NNR. 1,316 acres. Open water, reed and sedge beds, marshes, woodland, dykes, fen and carr. Public channel open to river craft. Bird watching facilities: 1 April – 31 Oct. On certain days to limited number of permit holders (fee payable). Obtain details from NNT, Norwich, well in advance of proposed visit. Unsold permits of a day's quota from Hickling Warden (9–9.30a.m.). 1 Nov. – 31 March: restricted facilities by advance application. Water trail: early June – mid-Sept. Wednesdays and Thursdays, 10a.m. and 2p.m., permits (fee includes brochure) obtainable at the Pleasure Boat Inn Staithe or from Warden. Car park for visitors to hides: follow Stubb Road from Greyhound Inn, Hickling Green. Follow the sign 'Marshes' and then take third turning on right. Meet Warden at Observation Hut, 250 yards W of car park near Whiteslea Lodge, 10a.m. or 2p.m. Booklet sold by NNT.

Holkham 26

E and W of TF 9044. North Norfolk coast. NNR. 4,200 acres coastal marshes and dunes (Burnham Overy – Stiffkey) and 5,500 acres inter-tidal sand and mud flats (Burnham Overy – Blakeney). PAR, refer NCCEA. Access to farmland between Burnham Overy and Wells is restricted. Access by vehicles: private road from Holkham village to foredunes. On foot: along sea wall from Overy Staithe or along beach from Wells and Stiffkey. Leaflet from NCCEA.

Holme Bird Observatory 27

TF 7144. North Norfolk coast: 2m E of Holme village. Independent observatory where Heligoland traps are used by qualified ringers. Thicket and pine-covered sand dunes. 6 acres. Open to visitors (April – November: daily; Winter: weekends), day permit charge to non-members. Access by road from A 149: take Holme beach road and then second right just before golf-course.

Holme Dunes 28

TF 7044. North Norfolk coast. NR, SSSI. 400 acres. Foreshore, sand dunes, fresh marsh, salt marsh. Bird Watching facilities: 1 April – 31 October (except Tuesdays): open to limited number of permit holders. Applications to NNT, Norwich, at least one week in advance (fee payable). Unsold permits of a day's quota from Holme Warden after 10a.m. 1 November – 31 March: restricted facilities by advance application. Nature trail: 1 May – 30 Sept. Open daily (except Tuesdays) to limited number of visitors (fee payable includes brochure). Access on foot along the Thornham sea wall. By car from A 149: take Holme beach road northwards, turn right just before golf course (car parking space indicated). Contact Warden at The Firs, 1m E of main entrance gate. Room for use of NNT members and visitors and limited dormitory accommodation for naturalists at The Firs. Brochure sold by NNT.

Horsey 29

TG 4522. Broadland and Norfolk coast: 2½m NE of Potter Heigham, 11m N of Great Yarmouth. NT. Mere, marshes, marrams, farmland. Access to Horsey Mere (120 acres) by boat. Restricted access to parts of 1,732-acre estate for naturalists (Apply Mr John Buxton, Horsey Hall).

Ickworth 30

TL 8161. Suffolk: 3m SW of Bury St Edmunds on W side of A 143. NT. House, garden and park. Access to house seasonal, admission fee. Park open daily, free.

Iken Cliff 31

Suffolk: 10m NE of Woodbridge. Picnic site approved by the Countryside Commission, managed by Suffolk County Council. 3 acres. Free access.

Kelling Park Aviaries 32

TG 0941. Norfolk: 2m from Holt on Weybourne Road. Pheasants, waterfowl, exotic tropical birds. Open daily. Admission fee. Free car park.

Kilverstone New World Wildlife Park 33

TL 8984. Breckland: On A 11, 1m Norwich side of Thetford. Collection of over 400 animals and birds. Deer park, wildfowl sanctuary. Open daily. Admission fee. Free car park. Picnic area.

Knettishall Heath 34

TL 9580. Breckland: 5m SE of Thetford, off A 1066. Country Park managed by Suffolk County Council. 178 acres. Free access.

Kyson Hill 35

TM 269477. Suffolk: ¾m S of Woodbridge, 1m E of junction of A 12 and B 1438. NT Open Space. 4 acres. Parkland overlooking River Deben. Free access.

Lynn Forest 36

TF 680105. Norfolk: Shouldham Warren, 6m SE of Kings Lynn on by-road running E from A 134. Picnic site, forest walk.

Mickfield Meadow 37

TM 143633. Suffolk: N of Mickfield and W of Greenwood Farm. SPNR reserve, leased to STNC. 4.6 acres. Undrained field, habitat of Snake's head (Fritillary). Access at all times to STNC members. Others need permit from STNC Secretary. Fritillaries should not be picked. Access by arable headland on S side of field adjacent to watercourse crossing road at foot of incline. Reserve is second field in from road.

Minsmere 38

TM 473672. Suffolk coast: 2m S of Dunwich. NR, RSPB. RWR. 1,528 acres. Marsh, lagoon, reed, heath and woodland. PVR, apply Permit Secretary, Minsmere Reserve, Westleton, Saxmundham, Suffolk IP17 3BY, having first obtained details of visiting arrangements and permit charges from January-February issue of *Birds* or RSPB. Follow same road as for Dunwich Heath (See above), cross heath, pass Coastguard Cottages and park on hill overlooking Minsmere. Walk S between sea walls to gate with notice (permit holders only). Binoculars may be hired. Public shore hide for non-permit holders S of entrance.

Norfolk Wildlife Park 39

TG 1118. Norfolk: Great Witchingham, on A 1067, 12m NW of Norwich. The Ornamental Pheasant Trust's collection and a large number of European animals and birds. Open daily. Admission fee. Free parking.

North Warren 40

TM 455587. Suffolk coast: Thorpeness. NR, RSPB. 196 acres. Heather, birchwoods and bracken. Open all year (no charge). No permit required, but access strictly limited to public footpaths.

Orford Beach 41

TM 4549. Suffolk coast: 1m S of Orford. Part of Orfordness-Havergate NNR and NWR. Large shingle spit with shingle beach vegetation. Permits are not required to visit, but no camping is allowed. Applications to carry out scientific work or to collect specimens to NCCEA.

Outney Common, Bungay 42

TM 3290. Suffolk: in a loop of the River Waveney, on NW side of Bungay. 495 acre common: NT owns six out of 300 undivided 'goings' or rights of pasturage. Access from Outney Road and Broad Street. Public footpath from Broad Street entrance across common to Ditchingham.

Ramparts Field, Icklingham 43

TL 7871. Breckland: 6m NW of Bury in Lark valley. Picnic place managed by Suffolk County Council. 17 acres. Valley slope with Scots pine and gorse. Free access.

Redgrave and Lopham Fens 44

TM 042795, 045795, 047799, 055800. Suffolk: 5½m W of Diss. STNC reserve, SSSI. 314 acres. Valley fen with varying habitats and conditions. Access at all times for STNC members. Non-members obtain permits from STNC Secretary. All visitors to sign book at Chequers Farm, South Lopham. From B 1113 take minor road ¾m S of South Lopham to entrace ½m along S side (small car park provided). STNC pamphlet available.

Rodbridge Park, Long Melford 45

TL 8543. Suffolk: 1m N of Sudbury, off A 134. Picnic site approved by the Countryside Commission, managed by Suffolk County Council. 18½ acres. Old mineral workings. Free acess.

Roydon Common 46

TF 6822. Norfolk: 4½m NE of King's Lynn, from which take A 149 and then A 148, turning right at Rising Lodge. NR, SSSI. 140 acres. Includes dry to wet heath, reed swamp, carr, fen and bog.

Sandringham Country Park 47

TF 6928. Norfolk: Royal Estate S of Dersingham, off A 149. Country Park approved by the Countryside Commission, managed by Sandringham Estate. 340 acres. Woodland, museum, picnic areas, car parks, information centre. Open April – Sept.

Scolt Head Island 48

TF 8146. North Norfolk coast: 3m N of Burnham Market. NNR. Shingle, sand dunes, salt marshes. Nesting areas (ternery) closed to visitors May – July. Access by boat 2–3 hours before and after high water in summer (Contact local boatman at Brancaster Staithe or Burnham Overy Staithe). Do *not* walk across the marshes to the Island unless accompanied by someone with real local knowledge. Nature Trail leaflet obtainable locally and from NCCEA. See book *Scolt Head Island* (edited Steers).

Snettisham 49

TF 648333. North Norfolk coast. NR, RSPB. Enclosed sanctuary pit with a public and a members' hide. No permits required, but parties over ten by prior arrangement with the Warden (School House, Wolferton, Kings Lynn, Norfolk PE31

6HD). Use the public car park: no parking on private road to reserve.

Suffolk Wildlife and Country Park 50
TM 5286. Suffolk: Grove Farm, Kessingland, 5m S of Lowestoft off A 12. Country Park approved by the Countryside Commission, managed by L. F. Wright. Collection of animals and birds. Open daily. Admission fee. Free car park. Picnic area.

Sutton Common 51
TM 2040. Suffolk: 3¾m SE of Woodbridge on B 1083. Picnic site approved by the Countryside Commission, managed by Suffolk Coastal District Council. 114 acres. Free access.

Swanton Novers Woods 52
TF 0130. Norfolk: 6m E of Fakenham. NNR. 147 acres. Ancient deciduous woodland. PVR, refer NCCEA (limited number of permits available for woodland research and other approved purposes).

Thetford Forest 53
83 square miles in Norfolk-Suffolk Breckland (Main centres: Thetford and Brandon). Forestry Commission pine plantations with broadleaved trees in roadside belts. Many forest walks, picnic places and public bridlepaths and footpaths. Visitors should have *Thetford Forest Guide Map* (Obtainable from Forestry Commission at Cambridge or Santon Downham).
ARBORETUM TL 823943. Near Lynford Hall.
INFORMATION CENTRE TL 816871. Santon Downham: on by-road 1½m NW of Thetford, 2m NE of Brandon.
LONG DISTANCE WALK Didlington High Ash (TL 813967) to West Stow (TL 815716): 22m.
PICNIC SITES AND FOREST WALKS/ TRAILS (PS = picnic site)
Bridgham Lane TL 968836 PS 3 walks.
Devil's Punchbowl TL 877893 PS 3 walks.
Emily's Wood TL 797895 PS.
Harling Drove TL 851892 PS.
Hockham TL 937919 PS 2 walks.
King's Forest TL 824755 PS Forest trail (starts at Forest Lodge, West Stow: TL 815715).
Lynford Long Water TL 818938 Forest walk.
Lynford Stag TL 813917 PS 4 walks.
Mildenhall TL 730745 PS.
Santon Downham TL 816878 Forest trail.
Swaffham Heath TF 777097 PS 3 walks.
Two Mile Bottom TL 852871 PS 3 walks.
WILDLIFE OBSERVATION TOWER Available by prior booking through Forestry Commission, Santon Downham.

Thetford Heath 54
TL 8579. Breckland: 2½m SW of Thetford. NNR.

250 areas. Heath-type communities. PVR, refer NCCEA.

Titchwell Marsh 55
TF 757437. North Norfolk coast. NR, RSPB. Saltmarsh, freshwater reedbed. No permits required. Access restricted to east sea-wall (use wooded path which joins A 149 between Titchwell and Brancaster) and west sea-wall (use track which joins A 149 midway between Thornham and Titchwell). Hide open May-July (approach from beach only).

Toby's Walk 56
TM 4474. Suffolk: about ½m S of Blythburgh on A 12. Picnic site approved by the Countryside Commission, managed by Suffolk County Council. 24 acres. Free access.

Walberswick 57
TM 4773. Suffolk coast: 1m S of Southwold. NNR. 1,260 acres. Heathland, woods, marshes, extensive reedbeds and mudflats. PAR, refer NCCEA. Good views of reserve from Blythburgh-Walberswick road and also from lane running W from Walberswick towards Westwood Lodge. Access to public rights of way across the reserve (See Reserve signs). NCC leaflet available.

Wangford Warren 58
TL 756842. Breckland: 2m S of Brandon. NR, SSSI. 38 acres. Relict fen and sand dunes. Access at all times to STNC members. Others consult STNC Secretary. Entrance at W side of A 1065, S of Northcourt Lodge.

Weeting Heath 59
TL 7888. Breckland: 1½m NW of Brandon. NNR. 343 acres. Typical example of a Breck-heath. April-July: hide permits (fee payable) from Warden's caravan, S of Weeting-Hockwold Road at W side of reserve. For access other than to hides: PVR, refer NCCEA.

Welney Wildfowl Refuge 60
TL 5494. Norfolk: Ouse Washes, between Old and New Bedford Rivers. Wildfowl Trust Refuge. 710 acres. Washland (winter floods) with wide lagoon and spacious observatory. Open to visitors all the year round (except Christmas Day). Admission charge to non-members. Escorted, unescorted, party and overnight visits. On arrival all visitors must call at Warden's Office, Pintail House, on SE side of Washes, 1¼m NE of Suspension Bridge. Special refuge leaflet from Wildfowl Trust, Slimbridge, Gloucester, or from refuge warden.

Wensum Forest 61
TG 318312. Norfolk: Bacton Woods, on by-road running S from B 1150 2½m NE of North Walsham. Forest walk.

Westleton Heath 62

TM 4569. East Suffolk coast 'Sandlings': 2m SW of Dunwich. NNR. 117 acres. Sandy and shingly heathland. PAR. Map on Reserve sign shows area beside Dunwich-Westleton road where car parking and picnicking allowed during daytime (tents and caravans not allowed anywhere on reserve). NCC leaflet available.

West Runton ('The Roman Camp') 63

TG 183414. Norfolk coast: ¾m S of West Runton station, between Sheringham and Cromer (A 149). NT Open Space. 71½ acres. Includes the highest point in Norfolk. Car parking. Free access at all times.

Winterton Dunes 64

TG 4920. Norfolk coast: 8m N of Great Yarmouth. NNR. 259 acres. Heaths, bogs and dunes. PAR, refer NCCEA. Access on foot. Car park at Winterton Beach. Leaflet from NCCEA.

Wolves Wood 65

TM 055440. Suffolk: 2m from Hadleigh on A 1071 to Ipswich. NR, RSPB. Open April-July inclusive. No permits required. Follow signposted footpath starting from large sign at reserve entrance.

The Country Code

1 Guard against all risk of fire.
2 Fasten all gates.
3 Keep dogs under proper control.
4 Keep to the paths across farm land.
5 Avoid damaging fences, hedges and walls.
6 Leave no litter.
7 Safeguard water supplies.
8 Protect wild life, wild plants and trees.
9 Go carefully on country roads.
10 Respect the life of the countryside.

Extract from The Broadland Code

1 NATURAL SURROUNDINGS

Take great care that you *avoid* damaging banks, shoreline vegetation and marshland. DON'T disturb nesting birds. *Avoid* shallow water where fish may spawn.

2 YOUR LITTER

Make sure that you use the litter baskets provided at recognised mooring and parking places and yacht stations. *Never* leave any litter about on land or water, take it home with you.

Be particularly careful how you dispose of plastic, cellophane, and other indestructible materials, they must never be left about as they can kill or maim wildlife.

3 POLLUTION

Do your best not to pollute the water or banks in any way and use public lavatories on shore whenever you can.

4 PRIVATE PROPERTY

Remember all the land adjoining the water belongs to someone. Please respect this ownership. Do not trespass.

Some useful addresses

BRITISH DEER SOCIETY
Headquarters: 17a East Parade, Leeds
LS1 2BU.
East Anglian Branch: Secretary: Mrs K. M.
Ross, 16a Edith Grove, Chelsea, London
SW10 0LN.

BRITISH TRUST FOR ORNITHOLOGY
Headquarters: Beech Grove, Tring,
Hertfordshire HP23 5NR.
Regional representatives: List issued to
members.

COUNTY TRUSTS FOR THE
CONSERVATION OF NATURE
NORFOLK NATURALISTS' TRUST
72 Cathedral Close, Norwich NOR 16P,
Norfolk.
SUFFOLK TRUST FOR NATURE
CONSERVATION
Estates Department, St Peter's House,
Cutler Street, Ipswich IP1 1UU, Suffolk.

FIELD STUDIES COUNCIL
Headquarters: 9 Devereux Court, Strand,
London WC2R 3JR.
Field Centre: Flatford Mill, East Bergholt,
Nr Colchester, CO7 6UL.

FORESTRY COMMISSION
Headquarters: 25 Savile Row,
London W1X 2AY.
East Conservancy: Government Buildings,
Brooklands Avenue, Cambridge.
Information Centre: Santon Downham,
Norfolk (on by-road $1\frac{1}{2}$m NW of Thetford,
2m NE of Brandon.)

MUSEUMS
NORFOLK
King's Lynn: Old Market Street.
Norwich: Castle Museum.
Sandringham: Sandringham Estate Museum.
Santon Downham: Forestry Commission
Museum.

Thetford: Ancient House Museum, White
Hart Street.
SUFFOLK
Bury St Edmunds: Moyse's Hall Museum,
Buttermarket.
Ipswich: High Street.

NATIONAL TRUST
Headquarters: 42 Queen Anne's Gate,
London SW1H 9AS.
East Anglia Regional Office: Blickling,
Norwich NOR O9Y, Norfolk.

NATURAL HISTORY SOCIETIES
NORFOLK AND NORWICH
NATURALISTS' SOCIETY
Castle Museum, Norwich NOR 65B, Norfolk.
SUFFOLK NATURALISTS' SOCIETY
The Museum, High Street, Ipswich, Suffolk.

NATURE CONSERVANCY COUNCIL
Headquarters: 19–20 Belgrave Square,
London SW1X 8PY.
East Anglia Regional Office: 60 Bracondale,
Norwich NR1 2BE, Norfolk.

NORFOLK ORNITHOLOGISTS'
ASSOCIATION (parent body to Holme Bird
Observatory)
Aslack Way, Holme-next-the-Sea,
Hunstanton, Norfolk.

ROYAL SOCIETY FOR THE PROTECTION
OF BIRDS
The Lodge, Sandy, Bedfordshire SG19 2DL.

SOCIETY FOR THE PROMOTION OF
NATURE RESERVES
The Green, Nettleham. Lincoln LN2 2NR.

WILDFOWL TRUST
Headquarters: Slimbridge, Gloucester
GL2 7BT.
Wildfowl Refuge: The Warden, Pintail
House, Hundred Foot Bank, Welney,
Nr Wisbech, Cambridgeshire.

Principal sources and suggestions for further reading

EAST ANGLIA: SUB-REGIONS AND RESERVES

1 Blackmore, M. (Editor). *The Nature Conservancy Handbook 1968*. H.M. Stationery Office, 1968.

2 British Association for the Advancement of Science. *A Scientific Survey of Norwich and District*. London, 1935. *Norwich and its Region*. Norwich, 1961.

3 Chatwin, C. P. *East Anglia and adjoining areas*. (British Regional Geology). H.M. Stationery Office, 1961.

4 Clarke, W. G. *In Breckland Wilds*. Cambridge, 2nd edition, revised by R. R. Clarke, 1937.

5 Edlin, H. L. (Editor) *East Anglian Forests*. (Forestry Commission Guide). H.M. Stationery Office, 1972.

6 Ellis, E. A. *The Broads*. London, 1965.

7 Forestry Commission. *Thetford Forest Guide Map* and leaflets *King's Forest Trail* and *Santon Downham Forest Trail*. Santon Downham Forest Centre.

8 Lambert, J. M. etc. *The making of the Broads*. (Roy. Geographical Soc. Memoir). London, 1960.

9 Martelli, G. *The Elveden Enterprise : a story of the Second Agricultural Revolution*. London. 1952.

10 The National Trust. Brochures *Felbrigg Woodland Walk, Norfolk* and *Dunwich Heath, Suffolk*. Blickling, Norfolk, 1974.

11 The Nature Conservancy Council (East Anglia Region). Brochures and leaflets. *Bure Marshes National Nature Reserve, Holkham National Nature Reserve, The Hoveton Great Broad Nature Trail, Scolt Head Island Nature Trail, Walberswick National Nature Reserve, Westleton Heath National Nature Reserve, Winterton Dunes National Nature Reserve*.

12 *The New Naturalist* (A Journal of British Natural History). No.6. East Anglia. London, 1949.

13 The Norfolk Naturalists' Trust. Pamphlets. *History of Cley Marshes, Cley Marshes Nature Reserve, Hickling Broad National Nature Reserve, Holme Nature Reserve, East Wretham Heath Nature Reserve, Norfolk Nature Reserves*.

14 The North Norfolk Conservation Committee. Brochure. *A guide to Nature Reserves on the North Norfolk Coast*.

15 Steers, J. A. (Editor). *Scolt Head Island*. Cambridge, 1960.

16 Suffolk Trust for Nature Conservation. *Guide to Reserves*. Ipswich, 1973. *Redgrave and Lopham Fen*. Ipswich, 1970. (See also nos. 19, 24, 27, 31, 34, 41, 59, 68–71).

TREES AND OTHER PLANTS

17 Brown, D. H. and R. M. The Lichens of Blakeney Point, Norfolk. *The Lichenologist*. **4**: 1 (1968).

18 Brown, D. H. and R. M. Lichen communities at Blakeney Point, Norfolk. *Trans. Norf. Norw. Nat. Soc.* **21**: 235 (1969).

19 Nicholson, P. The use of heather burning as a management technique for a Suffolk heathland. *Trans. Suffolk Nat. Soc.* **14**: 7 (1968).

20 Petch, C. P. and Swann, E. L. *Flora of Norfolk*. Norwich, 1968.

21 Pierce, C. W. and Ranson, C. E. The Conservation of roadside verges in Suffolk. *Suffolk Nat. Hist.* **15**: 376 (1971).

22 Salisbury, E. J. The East Anglian Flora. *Trans. Norf. Norw. Nat. Soc.* **13**: 191 (1933).

23 Swann, E. L. *Supplement to the Flora of Norfolk*. Norwich, 1975.

24 Watt, A. S. Studies in the ecology of Breckland. *Journal of Ecology*. Vol. **24** (1936) onwards. (See also nos. 2, 4–6, 15, 47, 48, 50, 60, 61, 63, 66–71). (A new Flora of Suffolk is in course of preparation).

BIRDS

25 Allard, P. R. White storks in Norfolk. *Trans. Norf. Norw. Nat. Soc.* **21**: 162 (1968).

26 Avian Predators Working Party. *Predatory Birds in Britain*. London, 1973.

27 *Birds*. Bimonthly magazine of the Royal Society for the Protection of Birds. (Contains news of, and visiting details for, reserves).

28 British Ornithologists' Union. *The status of birds in Britain and Ireland*. Oxford, 1971.

29 Buckley, J. and Goldsmith, J. G. Barn owls and their prey in East Norfolk. *Trans. Norf. Norw. Nat. Soc.* **22**: 320 (1972).

30 Buckley, J. and Goldsmith, J. G. The prey of the barn owl in East Norfolk. *Mammal Review*. **5**: 13 (1975).

31 Clarke, P. R. *An introduction and guide to bird watching in Norfolk*. Norfolk Ornithologists' Association, 1970.

32 Murton, R. K. *Man and birds*. London, 1971.

33 Newton, I. *Finches*. London, 1972.

34 *Norfolk Bird and Mammal Report*. Annual publication of the Norfolk Naturalists' Trust and the Norfolk and Norwich Naturalists' Society.

35 Norfolk Ornithologists' Association. Annual Reports.

36 Parslow, J. *Breeding birds of Britain and Ireland*. Berkhamsted, 1973.

37 Payn, W. H. *The Birds of Suffolk*. London, 1962.

38 Richardson, R. A. The godwits of Cley. *Trans. Norf. Norw. Nat. Soc.* (*Norfolk Bird and Mammal Report*). **21**:284 (1969); **22**:5 (1970); **22**:180 (1971).

39 Seago, M. J. *Birds of Norfolk*. Norwich, 1967.

40 *Suffolk Bird Report*. Published annually in no. 70.

41 Turner, E. L. *Bird watching on Scolt Head*. London, 1928. *Broadland Birds*. London, 1924.
(See also nos. 2, 4–6, 15, 62, 65, 67–71.)

MAMMALS

42 British Deer Society. Deer distribution survey 1967–72. *Deer*. **3**:279 (1974).

43 Chapman, D. and N. *Deer of East Anglia*. Ipswich, 1973.

44 Corbet, G. B. Provisional distribution maps of British mammals. *Mammal Review*. **1**:95 (1971).

45 Cranbrook, Earl of. Mammal Records. *Suffolk Nat. Hist.* **15**:46 (1969).

46 Cranbrook, Earl of and Payn, W. H. Distribution of deer in Suffolk. *Suffolk Nat. Hist.* **15**:123 (1970); **15**:222 (1970).

47 Ellis, E. A. Some effects of selective feeding by the coypu on the vegetation of Broadland. *Trans. Norf. Norw. Nat. Soc.* **20**:32 (1963).

48 Gosling, L. M. The coypu in East Anglia. *Trans. Norf. Norw. Nat. Soc.* **23**:49 (1973).

49 Mammals Working Party. *Predatory Mammals in Britain*. London, 1973.

50 Sheail, J. *Rabbits and their history*. Newton Abbot, 1971.

51 Society for the Promotion of Nature Reserves. *Focus on bats*. Nettleham, Lincoln, 1974.

52 Vine, A. E. Badgers in Norfolk. *Trans. Norf. Norw. Nat. Soc.* **22**:191 (1971).

53 Weir, V. and Banister, K. E. The food of the otter in the Blakeney area. *Trans. Norf. Norw. Nat. Soc.* **22**:377 (1972).

54 West, R. B. and Nicholson, P. The Suffolk otter survey. *Suffolk Nat. Hist.* **15**:452 (1971).

55 West, R. B. The Suffolk otter survey. *Suffolk Nat. Hist.* **16**:378 (1975).

56 White, D. A. Brown hares on Orford Beach, 1964–6. *Trans. Suffolk Nat. Soc.* **14**:49 (1968).
(See also nos. 2, 4–6, 15, 29, 30, 34, 62, 65, 68–71).

AMPHIBIANS AND REPTILES

57 Buckley, J. Amphibia and reptile records from Norfolk. *Trans. Norf. Norw. Nat. Soc.* **23**:172 (1975).

58 Smith, M. *The British Amphibians and Reptiles*. London, 1973.

59 Woolston, J. Winterton Dunes Nature Reserve – The natterjack toad. *Trans. Norf. Norw. Nat. Soc.* **21**:251 (1969).
(See also nos. 5, 6, 65, 67–71).

INSECTS

60 Barnes, H. F. *Gall midges of economic importance*. Vols. I–VII. London, 1946–56. Vol. VIII by Nijveldt, W., London, 1969.

61 Darlington, A. *The Pocket Encyclopaedia of Plant Galls in colour*. London, 1968.

62 Harding, P. T. (Part 2 with Welch, R. C.). A preliminary list of the fauna of Staverton Park, Suffolk. *Suffolk Nat. Hist.* **16**:232 (1974); **16**:287 (1974); **16**:399 (1975).

63 Pierce, C. W. Barberry Carpet Moth. *Suffolk Nat. Hist.* **15**:273 (1971); **15**:511 (1972); **16**:394 (1975).

64 Plowright, R. C. On the distribution of bumblebees in Norfolk. *Trans. Norf. Norw. Nat. Soc.* **21**:48 (1967).
(See also nos. 2, 4–6, 15, 67–71).

GENERAL

65 Fitter, R. S. R. *The ark in our midst*. (The story of the introduced animals of Britain). London, 1959.

66 Forestry Commission. Pamphlets. *See your forests* (*Southern England*); *Forestry Commission campsites*.

67 Nature Conservancy. *Monks Wood Experimental Station Report for 1969–71*. Abbots Ripton, Huntingdon, 1972.

68 Norfolk and Norwich Naturalists' Society. Transactions, Newsletters.

69 Norfolk Naturalists' Trust. Annual Reports, Newsletters.

70 *Suffolk Natural History*. (Transactions of the Suffolk Naturalists' Society).

71 Suffolk Trust for Nature Conservation. Newsletters.

Index

Figures in bold type denote pictures
This index should be used in conjunction with the lists on pp. 138–51